# TOP **10**
# DUBAI
## & ABU DHABI

LARA DUNSTON
&
SARAH MONAGHAN

EYEWITNESS TRAVEL

Left **An advertisement luring shoppers to buy Dubai's gold** Right **Windtowers along the Creek**

LONDON, NEW YORK,
MELBOURNE, MUNICH AND DELHI
www.dk.com

Design, Editorial and Picture Research,
by Quadrum Solutions, Krishnamai,
33B, Sir Pochkanwala Road, Worli,
Mumbai, India

Reproduced by Colourscan, Singapore
Printed and bound in China by Leo
Paper Products Ltd

First published in Great Britain in 2007
by Dorling Kindersley Limited
80 Strand, London WC2R 0RL
A Penguin Company

Reprinted with revisions 2008

A CIP catalogue record is available from
the British Library.

ISBN 978 1 4053 3340 5

Within each Top 10 list in this book, no
hierarchy of quality or popularity is
implied. All 10 are, in the editor's
opinion, of roughly equal merit.

# Contents

## Dubai & Abu Dhabi's Top 10

**The information in this DK Eyewitness Top 10 Travel Guide is checked regularly.**
Every effort has been made to ensure that this book is as up-to-date as possible at the time of
going to press. Some details, however, such as telephone numbers, opening hours, prices,
gallery hanging arrangements and travel information are liable to change. The publishers
cannot accept responsibility for any consequences arising from the use of this book, nor for
any material on third party websites, and cannot guarantee that any website address in this
book will be a suitable source of travel information. We value the views and suggestions of
our readers very highly. Please write to: Publisher, DK Eyewitness Travel Guides, Dorling
Kindersley, 80 Strand, London WC2R 0RL.

Left **The impressive Jumeirah Beach Hotel** Right **A desert dune drive**

Left **A windtower in Bastakiya** Right **Dubai Creek Golf & Yacht Club**

 **Key to abbreviations**
**Adm** admission charges

# DUBAI &
# ABU DHABI'S
# TOP 10

DUBAI & ABU DHABI'S TOP 10

# Dubai & Abu Dhabi's Highlights

*The Arabian emirates of Dubai and Abu Dhabi, the most rich and powerful of the seven city-states that make up the United Arab Emirates, offer the best of East and West – Arab culture, Bedouin heritage and Islamic architecture, alongside excellent shopping, sophisticated dining and luxurious hotels. Dubai is divided by its bustling Creek and skirted with white sand beaches, while Abu Dhabi is situated on a splendid Corniche.*

### 1 Dubai Museum

Set in a well-preserved fort, the Dubai museum, with its whimsical dioramas *(below)* and fascinating displays, provides a comprehensive introduction to the city *(see pp8–9)*.

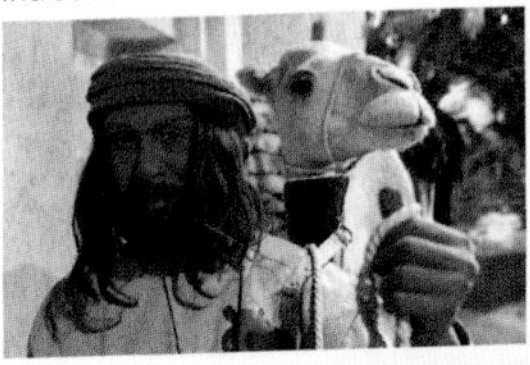

### 2 Dubai Creek

Criss-crossed by *abras* (water taxis) and *dhows* (old wooden boats) each day, this waterway *(below)* is Dubai's lifeblood *(see pp10–11)*.

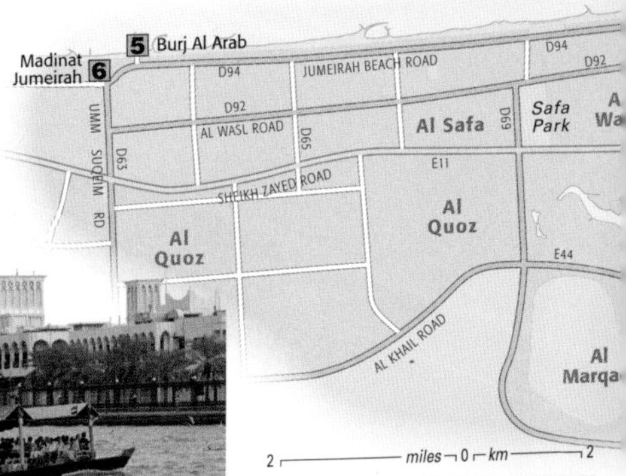

5 Burj Al Arab
Madinat Jumeirah 6
D94
JUMEIRAH BEACH ROAD
D92
UMM SUQEIM RD
D63
AL WASL ROAD
D65
Al Safa
D69
Safa Park
E11
SHEIKH ZAYED ROAD
Al Quoz
Al Quoz
E44
AL KHAIL ROAD
2 miles 0 km 2


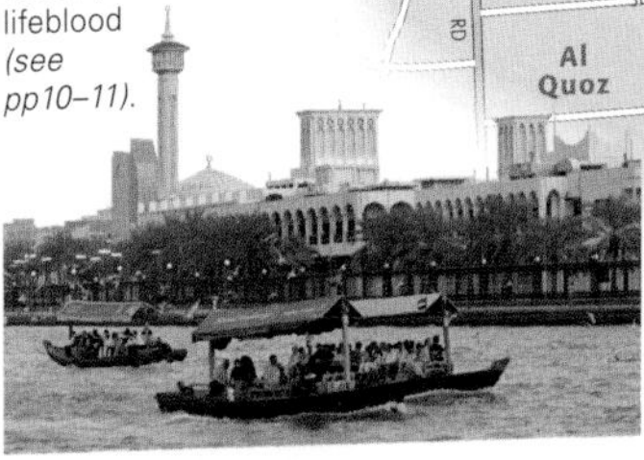

### 3 Bastakiya

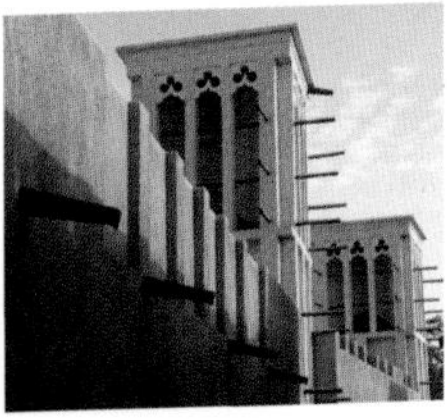

The gypsum and coral courtyard houses *(left)* in this quarter were constructed by Persian merchants who settled here in the last century *(see pp12–13)*.

### 4 Jumeirah Mosque

Not only is this mosque *(right)* Dubai's most beautiful, it's the only mosque open to non-Muslims. A guided visit to learn about Islam and culture is a must *(see pp14–15)*.

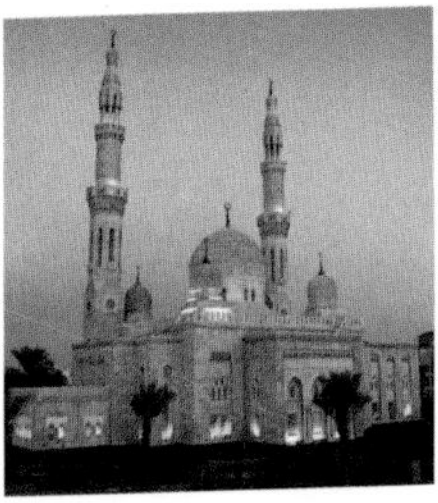

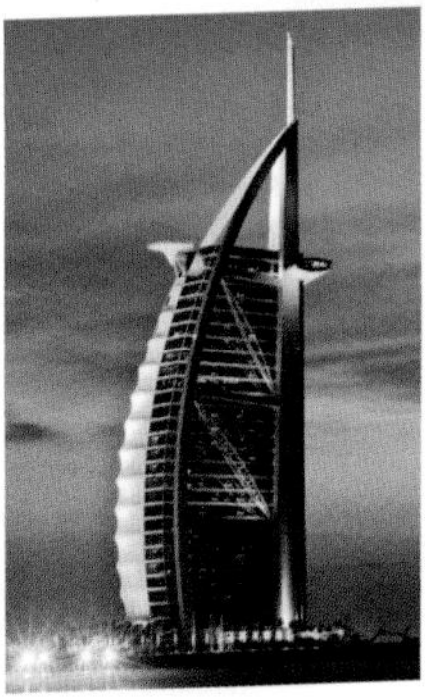

### 5 Burj Al Arab

This iconic, attention-grabbing "seven-star" hotel *(above)* is certainly a sight you cannot miss. It's the world's tallest hotel building *(see pp16–17)*.

*Previous pages* **The iconic Burj al Arab**

### Madinat Jumeirah (Dubai)
Shop for handicrafts, dine at a waterfront restaurant, see theatre or sip a cocktail as you enjoy the sunset at this Arabian-themed souq, entertainment and hotel complex *(see pp18–19)*.

### Dubai Souqs
Bargain for gold, perfume, spices and textiles, or simply take in the heady atmosphere of Dubai's souqs *(see pp20–21)*.

### Emirates Palace
The jaw-dropping display of gold lining the walls *(right)* and Swarovski crystals dripping from the chandeliers at Abu Dhabi's Emirates Palace hotel make for an impressive sight *(see pp22–3)*.

### Abu Dhabi Cultural Foundation & Al Hosn Palace
Enjoy the tranquil palm-shaded gardens of Abu Dhabi's elegant white fort palace *(above)* before taking in the handicraft displays and art shows at the Cultural Foundation *(see pp24–5)*.

### Desert Escapes
A visit to the UAE is incomplete without a desert experience. Stay at enchanting desert resorts Al Maha or Bab Al Shams or take a fun desert safari *(see pp26–7)*.

*To enjoy the highlights at a more relaxed pace, spend a few days in Dubai, a day or two in Abu Dhabi and a day in the desert.*

# Dubai Museum

*A visit to Dubai would be incomplete without a tour of this cleverly-planned museum. It offers a vivid picture of how Dubai has crammed into a third of a century what most cities achieve in several. Located near the creekside historic Bastakiya district, the museum is housed within and beneath one of the city's oldest buildings, Al Fahidi Fort. It traces the city's meteoric development from small desert settlement to centre of the Arabian world for commerce, finance and tourism. Visit here to gain a sensory insight into traditions past and present.*

### Top 10 Features

1. Al Fahidi Fort
2. Barasti Windtower House
3. Bedouin Traditions Display
4. Multimedia Presentation
5. Old Dubai Souq Dioramas
6. Islamic School Dioramas
7. Desert at Night Exhibitions
8. Underwater Pearl Diving Exhibition
9. Archaeological Finds
10. Wooden Dhow

*Bedouin wax figures*

🌀 A souvenir area sells traditional Bedouin artefacts, but it's more fun, and cheaper, to bargain in the souqs.

🖥 After your visit, retain the flavour of historic Dubai with lunch or coffee in the shady courtyard of nearby Basta Art Café *(see p71).*

- Map K2
- Al Fahidi Fort, Al Fahidi St
- 04 353 1862
- Open 8:30am–8:30pm Sat–Thu, 3pm–9pm Fri
- Adm
- www.dubaitourism.ae

### Al Fahidi Fort

**1** Originally built in 1787, this fort, with its magnificent watch tower, was constructed to defend the Emiratis against invasion. Renovated in 1971, it now serves as a city museum.

### Barasti Windtower House

**2** The fort's courtyard houses a *barasti* (date palm frond) home *(below)* and windtower cooling system, common in the region up to the 1950s.

### Bedouin Traditions Display

**3** A gallery displays the costumes, jewellery, weapons and tools of the Bedouin people. A holographic video presentation of a tribe performing the ceremonial sword dance, the *Ardah*, is hypnotic.

### Multimedia Presentation

**4** A 10-minute film presentation, with archive footage, explains the development of modern Dubai from 1960 onward. The film takes you through a pictorial tour of Dubai's transformation over 40 years, decade-by-decade.

### 5 Old Dubai Souq Dioramas

Holographic technology combined with waxwork figures *(left)*, smells, sounds and archive footage transport you into the creekside souq of half a century ago.

### 6 Islamic School Dioramas

Young Emiratis recite the lines of the Koran *(right)* under the eye of their tutor in this reconstruction of a 1950's school.

### Key to plans

| | |
|---|---|
| ▨ | Ground floor |
| ▨ | Basement |

### 7 Desert at Night Exhibitions

Learn how animals that live in the Arabian desert have adapted to cope with lack of water, extreme temperatures and shortage of food.

### 8 Underwater Pearl Diving Exhibition

This gallery explains the techniques used by pearl divers *(above)* who wore nose clips to descend to impossible depths.

### Bedouin Culture

*Bedu*, the Arabic word from which the name Bedouin is derived, means "inhabitant of the desert". Bedouins would move from oasis to oasis by camel and would engage in small-scale agriculture. The hardships of the desert have imbued Bedouin culture with a strong honour code and a famous hospitality.

### 10 Wooden Dhow

A traditional Arab vessel, the *dhow (above)*, is on show at the museum's exit. For celestial navigation, sailors used the *kamal*, a device that determines latitude using the angle of the Pole Star above the horizon.

### 9 Archaeological Finds

Interesting artefacts from excavations of graves that date back to 3,000 BC, such as fine copper and alabaster objects and pottery *(left)*, are on display.

# ☷10 Dubai Creek

*Dubai Creek, fed by the waters of the Arabian Gulf, is the lifeblood of old and new Dubai – a vibrant mix of the past and the present. The contrast of traditional wooden dhows being unloaded at the wharfage against stunning modern architecture, such as the glass dome-fronted Bank of Dubai (see p61) and the giant ball-topped Etisalat building, is fascinating. The two sides of the Creek are Deira (north) and Bur Dubai (south) and a walk along either is an enjoyable way to discover this multi-faceted city. Getting across the Creek is easy: the nearest bridge for cars is Maktoum Bridge but the cheapest and most authentic crossing has to be by abra.*

A creek cruise

🕐 By night illuminated *dhows* glide along the Creek.

🍹 Stop for a fresh juice at the stall at the entrance to the textile souq.

• Map K1–K6
• Abra Crossing: AED 1 each way • Creekside Park: 04 336 7633; Open 9am–8:30pm Sat–Thu, 3pm–8:30pm; Adm
• Sheikh Saeed Al Maktoum House: 04 393 7139; Open 8am–10pm, Sat–Thu, 3pm–10pm, Fri; Adm
• Heritage & Diving Village: Open 10am–midnight Sat–Thu, 4pm–midnight Fri • Bateaux Dubai: 04 399 4994; Open 8.30pm daily; www.bateauxdubai.com
• Al Mansour Dhow: InterContinental Hotel, Baniyas Road; 04 222 7171; departs 8.30pm • Creek Cruises: 04 393 9860; www.creekcruises.com
• www.dubaitourism.ae

## Top 10 Features

1. Abra Trips
2. Dhows
3. Waterfront Heritage
4. Wharf Walk
5. Bur Dubai Waterfront
6. Bait Al Wakeel
7. The Diwan
8. Creekside Park
9. Creek Cruises
10. Bateaux Dubai

### Abra Trips
*Abras* are flat-bottomed, open-sided water taxis *(right)* and are a breezy way to travel. Cram in with other passengers – the *abras* carry 40,000 people per day – and enjoy the great views.

### Dhows
The *dhow* is the traditional sailing vessel of the Emirates. These beautiful wooden boats *(left)* are used for tourist rides as well as for trade.

### Waterfront Heritage
In the Shindagha area near the Creek mouth you will find the restored house and museum of the late ruler Sheikh Saeed Al Maktoum and the Heritage and Diving Village *(below)*, which showcases Arabian culture.

### Wharf Walk
It's worth taking an amble alongside the colourful painted *dhows* moored on the Creek on Baniyas Road. They arrive each day from India, Iran and Oman. You can wander by and watch their interesting wares being unloaded.

### Bur Dubai Waterfront
The ruler's Diwan and historic architecture of "Old Dubai" can be enjoyed from the Deira side of the Creek *(above)*: windtowers, minarets and the domes of the Grand Mosque.

### Bait Al Wakeel
Built in 1934, this was the Dubai office of the British East India Company *(below)*. It has been completely restored and now houses a restaurant.

### The Diwan
With its modern white windtowers and imposing wrought-iron gates, the Diwan, or Ruler's Office, is impressive *(below)*.

### Creek Cruises
Several tour operators offer creek cruises with buffet lunch or dinner and entertainment on traditional wooden sailing *dhows*. A sunset trip is a treat, especially if accompanied by live belly-dancing and Arabian music.

### Creekside Park
A wonderful expanse of parkland, Creekside Park *(below)* stretches along the water's edge. Walk its length and enjoy the watery vistas or take a fun cable car ride from one side of the Creek to the other.

### Bateaux Dubai
An evening on the Creek aboard the sleek, glass-encased Bateaux Dubai is a luxurious way to enjoy the views. Four-course dinners, white table linen and live piano music make this a romantic indulgence.

### History of Dubai Creek
Once a tiny fishing settlement sprawled around the palm-fringed mouth of the Creek, Dibei, as it was known in the 16th Century, owes its existence to the 14-km (9 miles) Dubai Creek which led into a natural harbour and established itself as a flourishing hub for entrepôt trade.

# 🔟 Bastakiya

*The old and atmospheric Bastakiya quarter has benefited from extensive renovation work in recent years by Dubai Municipality. It gives a picturesque glimpse into the city's past in sharp contrast to the futuristic architecture and audacious construction projects elsewhere. Traditional sand, stone, coral and gypsum windtower houses, with elegant courtyards, can be explored as you wander the maze of shady narrow streets and alleys. The buildings have been restored to their original state, with Arabesque windows, decorative gypsum panels and screens. This area is now home to art galleries, museums and atmospheric cafés.*

*A Bastakiya window*

🌀 Set aside a couple of hours to fully see the Bastakiya quarter: late in the day, the golden light and long shadows add to the atmosphere.

⭕ For a light lunch, Basta Art Café offers healthy options such as fresh soups, salad and sandwiches.

• Map K2
• Sheikh Mohammed Centre for Cultural Understanding: 04 353 6666; www.cultures.ae
• Bastakiya walking tours: 10am Sun & Thu; Adm
• Basta Art Café: 04 353 5071; Open 10am–10pm Sat–Thu
• Bastakiya Nights: 04 353 7772; Open 12:30pm–11:30pm; DDD

## 1 Bastakiya History

Bastak, in southern Iran, is the origin of the name Bastakiya. It was traders from Bastak who founded this area by the Creek in the early 1900s. Drawn by Dubai's liberal tax policies, they settled here permanently.

## 2 Traditional Architecture

The need to remain cool prompted the distinctive vernacular style of the windtower courtyard houses *(right)*. Thick walls and narrow windows with intricate Arabesque designs are characteristic.

## 3 Al Fahidi Fort

Now Dubai Museum *(see pp8–9)*, this Fort *(above)* dates back to 1787. A sighting recorded in 1822 calls this "a square castellated building, with a tower at one angle... with three or four guns mounted".

## 4 Old City Wall

Restoration work of the original 200-year-old city wall *(below)* has reinforced the importance of this section of the original city as a crucial defensive zone.

### 6 Sheikh Mohamed Centre for Cultural Understanding

Established in 1999 to promote understanding of traditional Emirati culture and Islam, this centre offers walking tours, Arabic courses and cultural awareness programmes. The building is a stunning architectural example of a courtyard house.

### 5 Stamp & Coin Museum

Philately House *(above)* hosts an exhibition of the history of post and currency in the UAE. It explores postal activities before the federation was born.

### 7 Majlis Gallery

*Majlis* means meeting place in Arabic and this bijou art gallery, with a central garden area, is constructed around a beautifully converted whitewashed Arabic house *(left)*. Local Emirati and expat artists feature alongside original pottery, ceramics, crafts and jewellery.

### 8 Basta Art Café

Set in a traditional courtyard of a Bastakiya house, Basta Art Café *(below)* is a great spot to sit among flowering bougainvillea and enjoy lunch or a snack.

### 9 XVA Gallery, Café & Hotel

Enjoy contemporary art in galleries off the shady courtyard of this restored traditional house *(left)*. It also has a café and boutique hotel.

## Windtowers

Windtowers were the most distinctive architectural element of Arabic houses in the early 20th century. With four open sides, each of which was hollowed into a concave v-shape, wind-towers deflected the air down, cooling the rooms below. Water was thrown on the floor beneath the tower to cool the house further.

### 10 Bastakiah Nights Restaurant

This restaurant's *(right)* Arabian atmosphere is best experienced after dusk. The restored building has been traditionally furnished. Enjoy Arabic and Emirati food inside or on the rooftop.

# TOP 10 Jumeirah Mosque

*Dubai's culture is rooted in Islam, a fact that touches all aspects of everyday life. Virtually every neighbourhood has its own mosque, but the jewel in the crown is undoubtedly Jumeirah Mosque. This fine example of modern Islamic architecture was built in 1998. It is a dramatic sight set against blue skies and especially breathtaking at night, when it is lit up and its artistry is thrown into relief. Built of smooth white stone, the mosque, with its elaborately decorated twin minarets and majestic dome, is a city landmark and an important place of worship.*

*The mosque's interiors*

🅞 Opposite the mosque is Japengo Café: it's a pleasant spot for a drink or light lunch on the terrace.

✪ The mosque tours are intended to help visitors gain a real understanding of the Islamic faith, so make the most of the question time to find out what you would like to know. Photography is permitted.

---

• Map E4
• Beach Road, Jumeirah
• 04 344 7755
• Mosque tours: Sat, Sun, Tue and Thu, 10am, AED 50, no booking required
• Tel: 04 353 6666
• Sheikh Mohammed Centre for Cultural Understanding: www.cultures.ae
• Japengo Café: 04 345 4979, open 10am–1am, Sat–Fri

## Top 10 Features

1. Mosque Architecture
2. Minarets
3. Mihrab
4. Minbar
5. "Open Doors, Open Minds" Tour
6. Five Pillars of Islam
7. Prayers
8. Ramadan
9. The Haj
10. Mosque Etiquette

### 1 Mosque Architecture
With its vast central dome *(right)*, this mosque is inspired by the Anatolian style. The exterior is decorated in geometric relief over the stonework.

### 2 Minarets
Two minarets *(above)* crown this mosque. The height of the tallest one – the highest point of the "House of Allah" – is determined by how far the call to prayer should be heard.

### 3 Mihrab
The attractive *mihrab* – the niche in the wall of this and every mosque that indicates the *qibla*, the direction one should face when praying – gives the impression of a door or a passage to Mecca *(below)*.

### Minbar

The *minbar (above)* is the pulpit from which the *Imam* (leader of prayer) stands to deliver the *khutba* (Friday sermon).

### "Open Doors, Open Minds" Tour

The "Open Doors, Open Minds" interactive guided mosque tour run by the Sheikh Mohammed Centre for Cultural Understanding, offers an opportunity to admire the subtle interior decoration and to gain insight into the Islamic religion *(right)*.

### Five Pillars of Islam

The "Five Pillars of Islam" are: *Shahadah*, the belief in the oneness of God; *Salat*, the five daily prayers; *Zakat*, alms-giving; *Siyam*, self-purification and *Haj*, the pilgrimage to Mecca.

### Prayers

The *adhan* (call to prayer) rings out five times a day – all able Muslims must supplicate themselves *(below)* to Allah by praying on a *musalla* (traditional mat).

### The Haj

Every able-bodied Muslim is expected to make the annual pilgrimage to Mecca, in Saudi Arabia, once. Each year millions of Muslims from all over the globe do so to be forgiven of sins, to pray and to celebrate the glory of Allah.

### Ramadan

During the holy month of Ramadan, Muslims abstain from food, drink and other physical needs. This is a time for purification and to focus on Allah.

### Mosque Etiquette

Dubai may be cosmopolitan, but in keeping with mosque etiquette, you must dress conser–vatively to enter *(right)*. No shorts or sleeveless tops for either gender; women must wear a headscarf. Remove your shoes before entering.

### Call to Prayer

Wherever you are in Dubai, you are likely to be within earshot of a mosque and to hear the daily calls to prayer *"Allahu akbar"* (God is great). Today, the modern-day call is transmitted through loudspeakers; in the past the muezzin made the call himself.

*Dubai and Abu Dhabi's Top 10*

*Non-Muslims are not allowed to enter mosques, but frequent cultural visitor tours permit you to enter this mosque's interior.*

# 🔟 Burj Al Arab

*So iconic that it instantly became an international symbol for modern Dubai, the Burj Al Arab (meaning "Arabian tower"), completed in 1999, is an exclusive all-suite "seven-star hotel". With its helipad on the 28th floor and a restaurant seemingly suspended in mid-air, at a soaring 321 m (1,053 ft), it takes the trophy for being the world's tallest hotel. Set on its own artificial island against the backdrop of the turquoise waters of the Gulf, it is dazzling white by day and rainbow-coloured by night when its façade is used as a canvas for spectacular light displays.*

The Skyview bar

🕐 To visit the interiors, you must make a reservation for afternoon tea, cocktails or a meal. To do this, call 3017600 or email BAArestaurants@jumeirah.com

The dress code at the hotel means that you cannot wear jeans, t-shirts (collared shirts only), shorts, sandals (not in the case of women however), sports shoes or trainers.

- Map C1
- Jumeirah Beach Rd, Dubai
- 04 301 7777
- Cheapest entry: afternoon tea at Sahn Eddar (AED 190) or drinks package at Skyview Bar (AED 250 for 2 drinks and canapés)
- Al Mahara: Open 12:30pm–3pm, 7pm–midnight; DDDDD
- Skyview Bar: Open 11am–2am
- www.burj-al-arab.com

## Top 10 Features

1. Architectural Inspiration
2. Exterior Architecture
3. Design Details
4. Interior Architecture
5. Fish Tanks
6. Lobby
7. Underwater Restaurant
8. Skyview Bar
9. Spa & Swimming Pool
10. Suites

### 1 Architectural Inspiration
The billowing sail of the traditional Arabian *dhow* was the inspiration for this contemporary architectural creation *(right)*. Access is via the causeway Rolls Royces for guests or by helicopter.

### 2 Exterior Architecture
The shore-facing façade of the Burj is covered by a stretched translucent fabric. This is Teflon-coated woven glass fibre. It is the first time such technology has been used in this way in any building worldwide.

### 3 Design Details
The interior oozes with exotic opulence, from the shell-shaped reception desk *(below)* to the gold-leafed surfaces. The upholstery is a riot of patterns and geometric designs.

### 4 Interior Architecture

The vast gold columns and many layers of floors rising up *(left)* from the lobby give a dizzying sensation.

### 5 Fish Tanks

The lobby boasts two-storey high tropical fish tanks. Scuba divers are hired for the daily maintenance.

### 6 Lobby

The upper lobby is an airy space of marbles, mosaics *(below)* and carpets in swirling patterns. There is an impressive multi-hued dancing fountain.

### 7 Underwater Restaurant

Eating at Al Mahara is like taking a submarine voyage. Dine on fresh seafood and watch exotic fish glide by in the aquarium *(below)*.

### 8 Skyview Bar

This rooftop bar with its sky-high location offers spectacular vistas of the shimmering coastline. It is reached by an express panoramic lift. A must for cocktails at sunset.

### 10 Suites

The 202 duplex suites *(above)* are equipped with the latest remote technology, plus in-suite check-in and butlers. The two Royal Suites offer unsurpassed luxury, including a private cinema.

### 9 Spa & Swimming Pool

On the 18th floor is the Assawan Spa, a fitness facility with soothing ocean views. The decor is reminiscent of baths used by ancient Middle Eastern civilizations.

### The Construction

The Burj Al Arab is said to be one of the most expensive buildings ever constructed and the cost has never been revealed. 250 foundation piles were driven 40 m (132 ft) deep into the seabed; 70,000 cubic m (2,472,026 cubic ft) of concrete and more than 9,000 tons of steel were needed to construct the tower structure; 43,446 sq m (467,648 sq ft) of glass cover the building; 30 different types of marble and 8,000 sq m (86,111 sq ft) of 22-carat gold leaf are incorporated in the decor.

# 10 **Madinat Jumeirah**

*The spirit of old Arabia is the inspiration for Madinat Jumeirah, an extravagant complex located on the beachfront comprising two luxury hotels, Al Qasr and Mina A'Salam, and the exclusive Dar Al Masyaf, 29 traditional courtyard summer houses. The charm of the place lies in its detailed Arabian architectural styling – sand-coloured windtowers, arches, stairways and terraces – as well as its ingenious construction around a series of man-made waterways. As a result, navigation around the resort is Venetian-style, in old-fashioned abras. There is an Arabian-style souq, restaurants and bars.*

*Souq Madinat Jumeirah*

🧭 **If you get lost, ask for a resort map at any of the many information points. Guests can use a connecting board–walk to nearby Wild Wadi Water Park, Jumeirah Beach Hotel and Burj Al Arab.**

🅾 **For a real pick-me-up, try an espresso martini on the Koubba Bar terrace.**

- Map C2
- Madinat Jumeirah, Al Sufouh Rd, Umm Suqeim, Dubai
- 04 366 8888
- Jambase: Open 7pm–2am
- Koubba Bar: Open noon–2am
- Zheng-He: Open noon–3pm & 7pm–11:30pm

## Top 10 Features

1. Souq Madinat Jumeirah
2. Madinat Arena
3. Madinat Theatre
4. Central Plaza: live music
5. Al Qasr Hotel
6. Mina A'Salam Hotel
7. Talise Spa
8. An Arabian Venice: Canals
9. Canal-side Eating
10. JamBase

### 1 Souq Madinat Jumeirah
This souq is a beautifully recreated Arabian market-place and as it is air-conditioned, is a delightful place to browse. On sale are Arabian handicrafts, carpets and curios, all, however, at tourist prices.

### 2 Madinat Arena
Built around a lagoon, this multi-purpose amphi-theatre area *(below)* is capable of seating over 4,000. It is designed in the style of an old fortress. The encircling citadel houses shops and restaurants.

### Madinat Theatre
Host to the Dubai International Film Festival, the Madinat Theatre *(above)* – a 442-seat luxury venue – has provided this previously rather culture-starved city with a lively programme of opera, ballet, comedy and film.

### Central Plaza

Follow the meandering paths through the souq past open-fronted shops and galleries to the central plaza, where you'll find A'Rukn – a street café with an Arabic twist – the perfect place to enjoy coffee and sample shisha.

### Al Qasr Hotel

Al Qasr *(left)* is designed to reflect a Sheikh's summer residence. An opulent hotel, this quieter part of the whole complex is surrounded by water on a virtual island.

### Mina A'Salam Hotel

Built in the style of a mythical Arabian city, this sea-facing hotel *(below)* is home to lively eating and drinking venues. All the rooms and suites have balconies.

### Talise Spa

Relaxation is taken seriously in this tranquil oasis. The spa has 26 treatment rooms located on island clusters so you arrive by *abra*. Each treatment is described as "person-centric".

### Canal-side Eating

Many of the restaurants and bars have large terraces overlooking the tranquil waterways, making alfresco dining a delight thanks to Dubai's reliable sunshine. Zheng-He's terrace is particularly charming.

### An Arabian Venice: Canals

There's no doubt that the beautifully designed labyrinthine canals with *abras (above)* and *dhows* are magical and romantic. Only in the desert of Dubai could such a fantastic resort rise.

### Dubai International Film Festival

Madinat Jumeirah is host to the Dubai International Film Festival (DIFF) which has seen celebrities such as Richard Gere, Oliver Stone and Laurence Fishbourne converge for a celebration of movie magic. Morgan Freeman expects that the festival will become "big enough to rival Cannes" in the years to come.

### JamBase

This is one of Dubai's most eclectic music venues *(left)* where you can dine and dance. It is a stylish jazz bar and offers a rare chance to listen to great live jazz, blues and R&B.

# 🔟 Dubai Souqs

*Shopping in Dubai is a shopaholic's dream – there's almost nothing you can't buy here – but away from the air-conditioned marble-floored shopping malls is another experience: the souqs. Many of these, such as the gold, textile and spice souqs clustered beside the Creek, date back to Dubai's beginnings as a palm-fringed trading port. Exploring these through their warren-like alleyways is a delight and a visit to the UAE would be incomplete without spending time in at least some of these fascinating bazaars. Generally, each type of stall, be it spices, crafts, perfumes or clothing, are located close together, making it easy to spot a good deal. Bring cash and keep in mind that bargaining is expected.*

*Gold Souq's wares*

⭑ **Bargaining is expected in the souqs.** Start at half of the initial price, more if you dare, and haggle with a smile until you reach a compromise.

**Tax-free prices in Dubai tend to make luxury items such as CDs, perfume and electronic goods highly affordable.**

🖦 **There's a great choice of good-value Indian restaurants in the Bur Dubai souq area.**

*Most souqs tend to be open 10am–1pm & 4pm–10pm Sat–Thu, 2pm–10pm Fri*

• www.dubaitourism.ae

## Top 10 Features

1. Deira Gold Souq
2. Deira Spice Souq
3. Deira Perfume Souq
4. Deira Covered Souq
5. Naif Rd Souq, Deira
6. Bur Dubai Covered Souq
7. Bur Dubai Textile Souq
8. Karama "Souq"
9. Satwa "Souq"
10. Dubai Fish Souq

### 2 Deira Spice Souq

This tiny souq is a sensory delight. You can buy aromatic frankincense and myrrh (with charcoal burners for them), plus an array of spices *(below)* such as cloves, cardamom and cinnamon. Iranian saffron is good value, too.

### 1 Deira Gold Souq

This souq gleams with gold, silver and gems. Prices are competitive; dealers come in from around the globe and strict regulations are followed.

### 3 Deira Perfume Souq

Fascinating shops sell heavy exotic scents like jasmine, oudh, amber and rose and will also mix individual "signature scents". Traditional Arabian attars *(above)* are for sale alongside Western brands.

### 4 Deira Covered Souq
The Deira Covered Souq feels more Indian than Arabic, with a great medley of merchandise on offer including colourful and interesting textiles, spices, kitchenware, clothes and henna being hawked.

### 5 Naif Rd Souq, Deira
A kitsch faux desert fort houses this traditional-style souq *(below)*. You can find everything from cheap clothes and fake designerwear to children's toys and trinkets.

### 6 Bur Dubai Covered Souq
Beautifully restored, this creekside souq *(left)* is covered by an arched pergola. It makes for an atmospheric walkway lined with money lenders and little stalls.

### 7 Bur Dubai Textile Souq
Be warned, a visit here may prompt a visit to a tailor. Wonderful fabrics of every texture and colour imaginable from all over the world – silks, satins, brocades, linens and more *(above)*.

### 8 Karama "Souq"
This souq offers all kinds of "copy" items, especially watches and handbags. The quality of much of the merchandise, although fake, is astonishingly good.

### 9 Satwa "Souq"
This bustling street is a great place to rummage for cheaper products, such as fabrics, household items and electronics, as well as *majlis* cushion sets *(below)*.

### 10 Dubai Fish Souq
Hammour, a local fish, is worth a buy. Here you can also barter for fresh barracuda, giant crab *(above)*, lobster and other shellfish.

### Visit to a Tailor's
Dubai is a great place for tailoring, with textiles being so widely available. Various tailors' shops can be found around the Textile Souq, but also elsewhere in Satwa and Bur Dubai. Most will copy from an original item or photograph or you can select from an array of interesting pattern books.

# ᵀᴼᴾ❿ **Emirates Palace**

*Abu Dhabi's stupendous Emirates Palace hotel dominates the horizon. While its staggering size is impressive, the lavish interior is breathtaking, with gold, marble and crystal throughout. Owned by Abu Dhabi government and operated by Kempinski hotels, Emirates Palace was built over three years by the architects responsible for Claridge's in London. While the Burj Al Arab is touted as a "seven-star" hotel, a rating that doesn't exist, Emirates Palace classifies itself as just that, a "Palace", with the opulent furnishings of a royal palace, regal service and a palatial experience like no other.*

*The Triumphant Arch*

🚗 If offered a buggy ride while wandering the grounds, it would be advisable to take it, as Emirates Palace is situated on a million sq m (over 10 million sq ft) of land.

☕ For a coffee or afternoon tea, call into Al Majlis coffee lounge or the Viennese style café. For a full meal, try Mezzaluna or Sayad *(see p93)*.

- Map N6
- The Corniche, Abu Dhabi
- 02 690 9000
- Taxi; if driving, there's valet parking
- Open 24 hours
- reservations. emiratespalaces. kempinski.com
- www.emiratespalace. com

## Top 10 Features

1. The Triumphant Arch
2. Palace Gardens & Fountains
3. Gold-plated Lobby
4. Domes
5. Palace Suites
6. Swarovski Crystal Chandeliers
7. Petrified Palm Trees
8. Algerian Sand Beach
9. Emirates Palace Theatre
10. Majlis with Arabian Horse Mural

### **1 The Triumphant Arch**

Before entering Emirates Palace you'll be impressed by a majestic pink Triumphant Arch gate with a dome on top and a long and very grand driveway. The gate is usually closed. It is only opened for royalty and dignitaries on some special occasions.

### **2 Palace Gardens & Fountains**

The exterior of the palace *(above)*, incorporating traditional Arabian elements, is painted to reflect the variations in colour of the Arabian sands. It is beautifully enhanced by its landscaped gardens and spectacular fountains.

### **3 Gold-plated Lobby**

The opulence of the lobby's gold interior *(left)* is dazzling. Until Emirates Palace was built, Abu Dhabi was a modest city. This is the first time her wealth has been on display in such an ostentatious way.

### Domes
4 There are 114 domes here. The most stunning is the Grand Atrium dome *(above)*, decorated with silver and gold glass mosaic tiles and a gold finial at its apex.

### Palace Suites
5 Emirates Palace has 302 plush rooms and 92 sumptuously decorated Khaleej and Palace Suites. On the fifth floor are the high-security Presidential suites and on the eighth are suites designed especially for the Gulf Rulers. The Saudi suite even has its own barbershop.

### Swarovski Crystal Chandeliers
6 You'll notice the extravagant use of chandeliers *(above)* throughout the hotel – at Emirates Palace, they're used like light bulbs and appear to be sparkling everywhere.

### Petrified Palm Trees
7 There are 800 trees within the hotel. The date palm *(below)*, a national icon, is everywhere. Some of the palm trees, petrified to preserve their natural beauty, look real and are very impressive.

### Algerian Sand Beach
8 The white sand of the 1.3 km- (1 mile) long beach was imported from Algeria. A popular beach for swimming and cricket before Emirates Palace was built, it was felt the sand wasn't soft enough for royal feet!

### Emirates Palace Theatre
9 Emirates Palace has given Abu Dhabi its first theatre, the largest in the UAE, with programs such as the Russian Ballet, Arabic orchestras and musical shows like "The Spirit of the Dance".

### Majlis with Arabian Horse Mural
10 The most impressive of the many plush public spaces here is the *majlis* (meeting area). It has a blue ceiling with frescoes and a magnificent mural of Arab stallions.

### On a Scale Like no Other
The sheer scale of Emirates Palace impresses if nothing else. Ambassadors from 17 countries greet guests in the main lobby, and there are 170 chefs to keep you sated. There's no need to book or pay an entrance fee here. Simply show up and admire the structure.

 *Emirates Palace has a collection of some 1,002 chandeliers made with Swarovski's premier Strauss crystals.*

# Abu Dhabi Cultural Foundation & Al Hosn Palace

*Emiratis proudly refer to Abu Dhabi as the New York of the UAE and Dubai as its LA. They see the city as an intellectual and cultural centre (whereas Dubai is all about the glitz and glam). No two buildings exemplify this more than the Cultural Foundation and Qasr Al Hosn. The Cultural Foundation aims to make the UAE heritage and culture accessible to the city's residents and visitors; the historic Qasr Al Hosn is being converted into a museum.*

A plaster moulding

*A display of Islamic calligraphy*

🌀 **Pick up a copy of the program from the information desk for exhibition, performance and film listings.**

🌀 **In the Heritage Corner is a Bedouin tent where an Emirati serves coffee and dates.**

🌀 **Try to visit the Cultural Foundation in the evening when it's at its liveliest.**

• Map P3
• Airport Rd, City Centre, opposite Etisalat building • 02 621 5300
• Open 8am–3pm & 5pm–9:30pm Sun–Thu, 5pm–8pm Fri, 9am–noon & 5pm–8pm Sat
• info@cultural.org.ae
• www.cultural.org.ae

## Top 10 Features

1. Al Hosn Palace History
2. Al Hosn Palace Gate & Wooden Door
3. Al Hosn Palace Towers
4. Al Hosn Palace Gardens
5. Al Hosn Palace Interior
6. Interior Details
7. Cultural Foundation Architecture
8. Cultural Foundation Exhibitions
9. Delma Café
10. Heritage Corner

### 1 Al Hosn Palace History

Built in 1761, Qasr Al Hosn *(right)* is the city's oldest building. Former home to the Al Nahayan family, rulers of Abu Dhabi without interruption from the 18th century until today, it was used as the seat of governance until 1966.

### 2 Al Hosn Palace Gate & Wooden Door

The main entrance *(left)* to the fort is decorated with elegant Portuguese-style tile work that is typical of tiles found in the Islamic world. The large wooden door has a smaller door that was for daily use. It is embedded with protective black iron spikes.

### Al Hosn Palace Towers

The several towers (above) were once used to protect the palace. The most impressive is the round tower with the blue dome.

### 4 Al Hosn Palace Gardens

The simple yet pretty (and underutilized) palace gardens (below) are spread across several courtyards and are shaded by date palm trees. With their trickling fountains, during the cool weather, they make a wonderful place to rest and write a postcard.

### 5 Al Hosn Palace Interior

The elegant palace interior (below) has long light-filled corridors from which all the traditional high-ceilinged rooms are accessible. It will soon be opened to the public.

### 6 Interior Details

The interior is much as it was with intricately carved wooden doors, *mashrabiya* screens and old painted decorations featuring beautiful flowers and peacocks.

### 7 Cultural Foundation Architecture

The functional, concrete Cultural Foundation has an elegant colonnade designed to catch the breeze. The Islamic tiles are worth noting.

### 8 Cultural Foundation Exhibitions

Displays on musical instruments and history, regular performances of various arts and skills, exhibitions and thematic displays are held here.

### 9 Delma Café

Delma Café is a pleasant place for fresh juices, sandwiches and sweets. You just might bump into an Iraqi composer or a Syrian poet here.

### Cultural Preservation

Emirati culture is found in its many dances and songs, its rich tradition of oral storytelling, its religious rituals and its wonderful Bedouin heritage. The Cultural Foundation's mission is to preserve and promote Emirati heritage and it's a great place to learn about local culture.

### 10 Heritage Corner

The wonderful live handicrafts displays outside Delma Café provide a rare opportunity to see Emirati women practicing their traditional crafts (right), such as basket weaving, *saddu* (textile weaving) and *talli* (embroidery). You can also buy the items.

*Take a postcard or book along – the gardens are a lovely place to sit and relax for a while.*

# 🔟 Desert Escapes

*The Emirates' desert is sublime in parts and a trip here is incomplete without experiencing its myriad textures and colours. Not far out of the cities, camels graze on desert grass. If you don't have a 4WD and off-road driving skills, the best way to experience the desert is at the magical desert resorts Al Maha or Bab Al Shams, or on a popular desert safari. While desert safaris are touristy, they're lots of fun and allow you to tick off a range of experiences you otherwise wouldn't get a chance to do. If you have time, stay overnight, sleep under the stars and enjoy the silence.*

An Arabian camel

A magical desert sunset

🕐 Unless you want to experience the scorching heat for which the UAE is infamous, visits to the desert are best done in spring, autumn or winter – never summer!

• Al Maha Resort: Dubai – 04 832 9900; www.al-maha.com
• Arabian Adventures: Dubai – 04 303 8888/343 9966, Abu Dhabi – 02 691 1711; Open 9am–9pm; Prices start at AED 270; www.arabian-adventures.com
• Blue Banana: 800 222 6262; Half-day sandboarding for AED 780 for 4 people; www.bluebanana.ae
• Bab Al Shams Desert Resort & Spa: 04 832 6699; www.babalshams.com

## Top 10 Features

1. The Desert
2. Desert Safaris
3. Bedouin Tents
4. Dune Bashing
5. Sandboarding
6. Camel Riding
7. Belly Dancing
8. Bedouin Feast
9. Bab Al Shams Desert Resort & Spa
10. Al Maha Resort

### 1 The Desert

The UAE is all desert, apart from Al Ain's lush date palm oases, the Hajar mountains and rocky east coast. There are stunning dunes *(below)* dotted with camels on the roads to Hatta and Al Ain, but the most spectacular dunes are in the Liwa Oasis.

### 2 Desert Safaris

Tour agencies like Arabian Adventures organize exciting desert safaris. These may include an exhilarating desert drive in a 4WD *(above)*, falconry displays, sandboarding, a sunset camel ride, Arabic buffet and belly dancing.

### 3 Bedouin Tents

Traditional chocolate-coloured goat- and camel-hair tents dot the desert dunes in winter. Emiratis love to get away from the cities and take their children camping so they don't forget their heritage.

 *To avoid dehydration in the desert, drink plenty of water. Protect yourself from the sun by slathering on sunscreen.*

### Dune Bashing
Experience an exhilarating "dune bashing" session – a white-knuckle 4WD desert drive across the monstrous sand dunes.

### Sandboarding
Sandboarding – a sort of desert snowboarding – is a popular activity in the UAE. The picturesque rust-coloured sand dune "Big Red" on the Hatta Rd is a favourite venue.

### Camel Riding
Get up-close-and-personal with this local beast of burden. Nothing beats a camel ride *(above)* along spectacular dunes at sunset on a desert safari.

### Belly Dancing
Belly dancing is known as Oriental dancing in the Middle East. Try to pick up some moves from the dancer at the desert safari *(below)* – she may even pull you up for a shimmy.

### Bedouin Feast
Try a delicious Arabic buffet *(below)*, such as the Bedouin feast at Bab Al Shams' Al Hadheerah Desert Restaurant. Try local specialities including roasted baby camel.

### Al Maha Resort
Book a private and romantic tent-like luxury suite, and you get your own personal plunge pool with the golden desert as your "backyard".

### Bab Al Shams Desert Resort & Spa
The palm-shaded gardens and trickling ponds make this desert resort *(below)* enchanting. A wonderful infinity pool overlooks the desert. Enjoy falconry here.

### Liwa Oasis
The most spectacular desert scenery can be enjoyed at Liwa Oasis, just a few hours drive from Abu Dhabi. The sand dunes of the Liwa are the prettiest-coloured, in shades of peach and apricot. They are also the largest in the UAE – best appreciated shortly after sunrise or sunset.

*Following pages:* **Camels being led across the desert sands**

Left **Camels grazing in the desert** Right **Henna application**

# ☺10 Culture & Tradition

### 1 Bedouin Society
The semi-nomadic lifestyle of the Bedu tribes – most of whom spent the harsh summers inland at the cool date-palm oases and their winters fishing by the sea – is a source of pride for Emiratis. ◈ *Visit the Heritage Villages in Dubai (see p67) and Abu Dhabi (see p89) for a glimpse into the Bedouin culture.*

### 2 The Camel
Mainstay of the Bedouin's nomadic life, the camel enabled tribes to move their possessions from coastal villages to inland oases. Camel's milk quenched their herders' thirst when water wasn't found, while the fur was used to make tents, textiles, rugs, bags and cloaks. ◈ *Ride a camel at the Heritage and Diving Village in Dubai (see p67).*

### 3 The Arabian Horse
Beloved by the Bedouin for their elegance and valued for their strength and sturdiness, the Arabian horse is one of the world's oldest and purest of breeds due to the Bedouin's careful inbreeding, practiced for centuries. ◈ *Appreciate the beauty of the Arabian horse on display at the Heritage and Diving Village (see p67) during Eid and Shopping Festivals.*

### 4 Falconry
In the past, falcons were used by Bedu to capture small birds and hares. Today, Emirati men still train their falcon daily.

Some desert resorts and safaris display falconry. ◈ *Dubai Falcon Centre: Nad Al Sheba; open 8:30am–8:30pm Sat–Thu, 2pm–8:30pm Fri*

### 5 The Date Palm
Dates were essential for desert survival. They were used to create *tamr*, a preserve, which helped sustain the Bedu over long journeys. There are over 50 date varieties in the UAE. ◈ *Bateel (see p37) sells good dates.*

### 6 Fishing and the Dhow
Historically, fishing, *dhow* building and pearl diving were the main occupations along the coastal settlements. Today, Emiratis still use the old wooden *dhow* boats for fishing, trading and tours. ◈ *Visit dhow-building wharves in Abu Dhabi (see p90).*

### 7 Poetry, Dance & Song
Emirati poetry takes many forms, from the romantic *baiti* style to the vernacular *nabati*

**An Emirati wedding procession**

*Camel's milk is more nutritious than cow's milk. You can buy it at the local supermarkets in Dubai and Abu Dhabi.*

**An Emirati with his falcon**

poetry. Wedding processions are an occasion for song and dance. Songs and group dances such as the *ayyalah* and *liwa* celebrate bravery in war and at sea. ◈ *Enjoy traditional performances at the Heritage and Diving Village (see p67) during Eid and the Dubai Shopping Festival.*

### Rifle-throwing

Prior to Federation there was periodic warring between tribes, and Bedu were respected for how they handled weapons. These days, young Emirati men practice throwing their rifles high in the air while dancing and clapping. ◈ *Watch gun-throwing competitions at the Heritage and Diving Village (see p67) during Eid and the Dubai Shopping Festival.*

### Traditional Dress

Women wear a black cloak-like *abaya* and black *shayla* to cover their hair. Men wear a white *dishdasha* and a white or checked *gutra* (head scarf) with a black *agal* to hold it in place.

### Henna

Intricate henna patterns were painted on pottery across the Middle East in Neolithic times, around 9000 BC. Today, Emirati women have henna designs painted on their hands and feet for weddings and other celebrations. ◈ *Get henna designs at "henna tents" in shopping malls.*

## Moments in History

**1 5000 BC: Abu Dhabi settlement**
Date stones on Dalma Island and flint tools on Merawah Island attest to human life in Abu Dhabi in 5110 BC.

**2 AD 700: Islam arrives**
The Umayyads bring Islam and Arabic to Arabia.

**3 1507: European traders reach the Gulf**
Portuguese invasion of Gulf islands and the east coast paves way for British, French and Dutch trading ships.

**4 1793: Al Bu Falah tribe settles in Abu Dhabi**
Al Bu Falah and Al Nahayan tribes settle in Abu Dhabi.

**5 1833: Al Maktoum tribe arrives in Dubai**
Under leadership of Maktoum bin Buti Al Maktoum, Al Maktoum tribe settles at the mouth of Dubai Creek.

**6 1894: Tax-free trading**
Dubai first introduces tax exemptions for foreigners. The Persians are the first expats.

**7 1930s: Pearling trade collapses**
The Gulf pearling trade collapses when the Japanese develop cultured pearling.

**8 1950s: Discovery of oil**
Oil is discovered in Abu Dhabi in 1958 and Dubai in 1966, changing fortunes.

**9 1971: UAE established**
UAE Federation forms from the seven emirates, with Sheikh Zayed bin Sultan Al Nahayan, ruler of Abu Dhabi, as President.

**10 2004: Death of Sheikh Zayed**
UAE goes into mourning with the death of visionary leader Sheikh Zayed, and in 2006, the death of Sheikh Maktoum.

 *When Marco Polo visited Dubai in 1580, he described it as a bustling seaport that was rich from its trade in pearls.*

Left **Dolphins near Saadiyat Island** Centre **Sir Baniyas Island** Right **The World project**

# 🔟 Audacious Projects

## 1 Sir Baniyas Island

This secret cone-shaped island in the Arabian Gulf is an extraordinary "ark" and conservation project. If you are lucky, you may spot some African giraffes and ostriches, llamas from Peru and even catch a glimpse of the Arabian oryx.
🔕 *Off the Abu Dhabi coast•* 02 444 0444
• *Visitor numbers are restricted*
• *www.exploreabudhabi.ae*

## 2 The Palms (Jumeirah)

This palm-shaped island may qualify for the "Eighth Wonder of the World" tag. It is one of the largest man-made developments and is visible from space. Housing close to 5,000 villas and luxury apartments (all sold out!), it boasts of resident celebrities. Two even bigger palm island projects, Palm Jebel Ali and Palm Deira, are under construction.
🔕 *Map B1 • Dubai • www.thepalm.ae*

## 3 The World

This grand project involves a marine development of 300 artificial islands 2 miles (4 km) offshore, designed in the shape of the world map. Buyers can take their pick of "countries"; prices range from $10–45 million. 326 million cubic metres of sand were required for land reclamation and a 17-mile (26 km) oval-shaped breakwater is being built. 🔕 *Map C1–D1 • Dubai*
• *www.theworld.ae*

## 4 Ski Dubai

The largest indoor snow park in the world, this cavernous space contains 6,000 tonnes of manufactured snow. Five runs vary in difficulty, the longest being almost a quarter of a mile (400 m), making it the world's first indoor black run. 🔕 *Map C2*
• *04 341 0010 • Mall of the Emirates, Al Barsha, Dubai • www.skidxb.com*

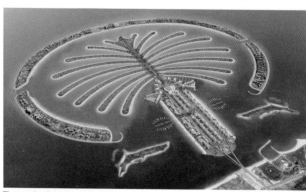

**The amazing Palm Jumeirah project**

### Dubailand

**5** Conceived on a phenomenal scale, with completion in 2020, this $4.5-billion development will be the biggest entertainment attraction on the planet, twice the size of the Walt Disney World Resort. Under construction are six enormous themed areas as well as a giant wheel that will permit a view of up to 31 miles (50 km). ⚲ *Map C3 • Dubai • www.dubailand.ae*

### Mall of Arabia

**6** The Mall of Arabia is set to open in 2008. Shoppers will be spoilt for choice, with more than 1,000 stylish international retail outlets and parking for 10,000 vehicles planned, making this the world's largest retail development. ⚲ *Map C3 • Dubai • www.cityofarabia.ae*

### Dubai Festival City

**7** A "city within a city", this huge waterfront lifestyle resort will extend 2 miles (4 km) along the Creek. It comprises a mind-boggling 20,000 homes, with schools, malls, hotels, a marina, 90 waterside restaurants, event and leisure facilities, including a golf course. When complete, 100,000 people will live and work here. ⚲ *Map E3 • Dubai • www.dubaifestivalcity.com*

### Burj Dubai & Business Bay

**8** Business Bay, the main business address for the Middle East, is soon set to open its dozens of skyscrapers to international companies. The area is home to the Middle East's "Wall Street", the Dubai International Finance Centre and the Burj Dubai, the world's tallest tower, expected to be almost half a mile (1 km) high – the precise figure is secret in case New York's Freedom Tower tries to top it! ⚲ *Map C6 • Dubai*

**Space & Science World in Dubailand**

### Dubai Infrastructure

**9** With so much development planned for the near future, the city's transport infrastructure will be crucial. Underway are three important projects. The first is the Dubai Metro, an under- and overground railway that, by 2020, will be able to handle 1.8 million passengers a day. The second is an expansion of the Dubai International Airport, with a new exclusive terminal for Emirates (Dubai's airline) and a cargo "mega-terminal". The third is a new six-runway freight-focused airport on the city outskirts at Jebel Ali.

### Saadiyat Island

**10** Set to become a major tourist destination for Abu Dhabi, this island is scheduled for completion in 2018. It will be home to some 150,000 people and this cultural hub will boast many world-class museums, including the Guggenheim Abu Dhabi, to be designed by Frank Gehry, a branch of the Louvre *(see p91)*, and a Biennale Park with 19 pavilions.

Left **Exhibition at B21** Centre **Pop art at Art Space** Right **The Third Line gallery**

# Art Galleries

### 1 The Third Line
This sleek gallery shows provocative and playful work by artists from around the Gulf. Exhibitions change every few weeks, launched by champagne openings. ◈ *Map C2 • Al Quoz industrial area, off Interchange 3, Dubai • 04 341 1367 • Open 11am–8pm Sat–Thu; Call ahead • www.thethirdline. com*

### 2 XVA
This superb art gallery is set in a stylish boutique hotel in a restored traditional house. Its courtyard café is also used as an exhibition space *(see p13)*.

### 3 Majlis Gallery
Dubai's oldest commercial art gallery focuses on Arabian and Middle Eastern themed work. Browse for good prints, ceramics and sculpture here *(see p13)*.

### 4 Art Space
With a mission to nurture local talent, this gallery has hosted great exhibitions by Middle Eastern and Emirati artists, like Mohammed Kanoo's playful pop art *(see p74)*.

### 5 B21
Check out the provocative paintings, photography and mixed media predominantly by Middle Eastern artists. Standout shows include Iranian photo-grapher-painter Shadi Ghadirian's "Like Everyday" series of women wearing bold patterned burqas with kitchen utensils in place of their faces. ◈ *Map C2 • Al Quoz industrial area, off Interchange 3, Dubai • 04 340 3965 • Open 11am–7pm Sat–Thu • www.b21gallery.com*

### 6 The Courtyard: Total Arts and The Courtyard Gallery
The highlights at this rather whimsical-looking Mediterranean-style complex are two wonderful galleries – Dariush Zandi's Total Arts at the Courtyard and Samia Saleh and Louis Rady's lovely Courtyard Gallery and Café. ◈ *Map C2 • Al Quoz industrial area, off Interchange 3, Dubai • Total Arts 04 347 0909; The Courtyard Gallery 04 347 5050 • www.courtyard-uae.com*

### 7 Green Art Gallery
Set in a modern minimalist white villa, this established commercial gallery showcases the work of Emirates-based as well as international artists who

**An exhibit at XVA**

Check out the exhibition calendar on www.canvasonline.com for art exhibitions in the UAE

**Art exhibition at Five Green**

are inspired by the heritage, cultures and environment of the Middle East. There is a season of changing exhibitions from October to May. ⓢ *Map C4 • Street 51, Jumeirah, behind Dubai Zoo • 04 344 9888 • Open 9:30am–1:30pm & 4:30–8:30pm Sat–Thu • www.gagallery.com*

**Five Green**

This funky fashion concept store frequently hosts local and global contemporary art. Don't be surprised if you walk out with a new outfit, magazines and a painting *(see p70)*.

**Folklore Gallery**

Folklore can't be compared to Dubai's slick galleries, but among the watercolours of desert landscapes leaning against the walls, you're sure to find some real gems at good prices. ⓢ *Map P3 • Zayed 1st St, Khalidiya, Abu Dhabi • 02 666 0361 • Open 9:30am–1:30pm & 5–10pm Sat–Thu*

**Hemisphere Gallery**

Abu Dhabi's best art gallery is set in the most unlikely area, among the shops and laundries around the Russian embassy. It exhibits a variety of styles by expat artists and also runs painting courses and workshops. ⓢ *Map P2 • Off Khalifa St, near Russian Embassy, Abu Dhabi • 02 676 8641 • Open 9:30am–1:30pm & 3pm–9pm Sat–Thu*

## Top 10 Festivals & Events

**1 Dubai Shopping Festival**
Sales and shows. ⓢ *Citywide • Dec–Feb • www.mydsf.com*

**2 Global Village**
Multicultural bazaar and fun fair. ⓢ *Map C3 • Dubailand, Emirates Road • Dec–Feb 4pm–midnight • www.globalvillage.ae*

**3 Dubai International Film Festival**
Glam galas and film screenings. ⓢ *Map C2 • Madinat Jumeirah, Um Suqueim, Dubai • Dec • www.dubaifilmfest.com*

**4 Dubai International Jazz Festival**
Global jazz gigs on the grass. ⓢ *Map B2 • Dubai Media City, Um Suqueim, Dubai • Mar • www.dubaijazzfest.com*

**5 Dubai Marathon**
Compete or simply run for fun! ⓢ *From Sheikh Zayed Rd to Jumeirah Beach Rd • Jan • www.dubaimarathon.org*

**6 Dubai World Cup**
World's richest horse-racing cup. ⓢ *Map D3 • Nad Al Sheba racetrack, Dubai • Feb–Mar • www.dubaiworldcup.com*

**7 Dubai Desert Classic**
Renowned golf players participate. ⓢ *Map B2 • Mar • www.dubaidesertclassic.com*

**8 Dubai Tennis Championships**
Catch the top tennis seeds in action. ⓢ *Feb–March • www.dubaitennischampionships.com*

**9 Dubai Summer Surprises**
A summer full of events for families. ⓢ *Citywide • 21 Jun–31 Aug • www.mydsf.com*

**10 UAE Desert Challenge**
A demanding 4-day motor rally through the desert.

Left **The amazing Ibn Battuta Mall** Right **Abu Dhabi's Marina Mall**

# Shopping Malls & Souqs

### 1 Mall of the Emirates
Over 300 stores, including a swish Harvey Nichols, make this the city's most sumptuous mall. If you're in a rush, use the mall's website to create an itinerary identifying the most direct route to the shops you wish to visit *(see pp78–81)*.

### 2 Bur Juman Mall
This glamorous mall houses exclusive designer stores such as Chanel, Dior and Kenzo, and jewellers like Cartier and Tiffany. There's a Sax Fifth Avenue, the second largest outside the USA, and shops selling books, music, perfumes and cosmetics *(see p70)*.

### 3 Deira City Centre
This mall may not be as spectacular as the newer shopping centres, but it's a local favourite. While you'll find all the usual Dubai stores here, most visitors come mainly for the excellent people watching *(see p62)*.

### 4 Emirates Towers Boulevard
This elegant shopping centre is packed with style gurus such as Georgio Armani, Gucci, Pucci and Jimmy Choo. But Villa Moda is the most chic of all, with its niche cosmetics and coveted brands such as Chloe and Miu Miu. ◈ *Map D6 • Sheikh Zayed Rd, Dubai • 04 319 8999 • Open 9am–10pm Sat–Thu, 2pm–10pm Fri*

### 5 Ibn Battuta Mall
One look at the five themed malls within this mall and you won't regret your long drive! The decor for each is inspired by the countries that Arabia's own Marco Polo, Ibn Battuta, travelled to: Tunisia, Egypt, Persia, India and China *(see p82)*.

### 6 Abu Dhabi Mall
You'll find a gamut of global franchises here as well as delightful local shops, from date sellers Bateel to boutiques selling Emirati national dress and sandals *(see p92)*.

### 7 Marina Mall
This glamorous mall has over 300 shops and a new extension adding even more. Expect big name brands, exclusive stores such as Rolex and Tiffany & Co, and traditional Arabian perfume, sweets and clothes shops.

**The posh interiors of Bur Juman**

*For Emiratis, shopping malls are about socializing as much as they are about shopping.*

**Perfume bottles at Deira City Centre**

There's an excellent range of cafés including Hediard from Paris (see p92).

### 8 Madinat Zayed Shopping Centre & Gold "Souq"
The nights are the liveliest at the Shopping Centre, home to global brands and local speciality shops. The glitzy Gold Centre, or new Gold "Souq", specializes in jewellery and watches (see p92).

### 9 Iranian Souq
This low-key souq specializes in kitchenware and garden plants, as well as decorative crafts, souvenirs and rugs from Iran (see p92).

### 10 Fish and Fresh Produce Souq
These markets are worth a visit just to take in the atmosphere. It's fascinating to find out where the fresh fruit and vegetables come from. Learn the Arabic words for your favourite fish and other seafood. ⊗ Map N1 • Port ("Mina" in Arabic), Abu Dhabi • Open 6am–late, quiet during prayer times

## Top 10 Shops

### 1 Damas
Visit the Gulf's largest jeweller for a huge selection of dazzlers (see p62).

### 2 Paris Gallery
This store has an enticing array of make-up and perfume at bargain prices (see p62).

### 3 Plug-ins
A digital and electronics retailer – the first stop for gadget lovers (see p62).

### 4 Bateel
Buy date goodies such as chocolate-coated dates or date jam as gifts. ⊗ Map J3 • Bur Juman Mall, Sheikh Khalifa Bin Zayed Rd, Dubai • 04 355 2853

### 5 Villa Moda
An elegant place for exclusive designerwear, from Alexander McQueen to Stella McCartney (see p36).

### 6 Mumbai Se
A must-visit for glam Bollywood-style fashion. ⊗ Map A2 • Ibn Battuta Mall, Sheikh Zayed Rd, Dubai • 04 366 9855

### 7 Azza Fahmy Jewellery
Inimitable jewellery combining Arabic calligraphy and Islamic motifs. ⊗ Map D6 • Jumeirah Emirates Towers Boulevard, Sheikh Zayed Rd, Dubai • 04 330 0340

### 8 Amzaan
Creative Dubai designers share space with hip foreign labels (see p70).

### 9 Sauce
You'll love the chic accessories and fashion. ⊗ Map D4 • Village Mall, Jumeirah Rd, Dubai • 04 344 7270

### 10 Five Green
Check out the edgy art, music, magazines and cool streetwear (see p70).

Get Alef magazine, the Emirati Vogue, when you arrive in town for more on local fashion.

Left **Dazzling gold bangles** Centre **Arabian antique lamp** Right **Beautiful designer textiles**

# 🔟 Things to Buy

### 1 Gold
Dubai is "the City of Gold". The Gold and Diamond Park glitters with ornate jewellery. Gold is sold by weight; intricate designs are more expensive. ⓢ *Map C2 • Sheikh Zayed Rd, Interchange 4, Dubai • 04 347 7788 • Open 10am–10pm Sun–Thu, 10am–midnight Sat–Fri • www.goldanddiamondpark.com*

### 2 Carpets
The UAE is the best place to buy Persian carpets outside of Iran. A discerning market ensures the best quality rugs come here while no tax keeps prices low. Shop around and bargain hard but most of all, enjoy the tea – the ritual is half the fun of it.

### 3 Arabian "Antiques" & Handicrafts
Arabian "antiques" include brass coffee pots, engraved trays and framed *khanjars* (daggers). You'll also find traditional Emirati handicrafts such as woven baskets, embroidery and red striped textiles made into camel bags and rugs. Moroccan lanterns, Turkish and Persian miniature paintings and Indian cushion covers are also popular.

### 4 Arabian Attars & Perfumes
The heady aromas of exotic Arabian *attars* (perfume oils) are an acquired smell. Many women buy them for the beautiful jewel-encrusted bottles. If offered *oud* (fragrant wood) in an incense

**Traditional Bedouin jewellery**

burner, don't forget to waft the smoke under your arms – it is used traditionally as a deodorant.

### 5 Bedouin Jewellery
Much of the old silver Bedouin jewellery comes from Oman, Yemen, Afghanistan and India, but only experts can tell. Expect to find chunky bangles, necklaces, earrings and rings, engraved and intricately set with gemstones, cowrie shells and dangling little bells.

### 6 Pink Sushi Designs
This local label features cute handbags and quirky skirts made using the *gutra*, the red and white checked Emirati head-dress. They are available from various stores, including Amzaan *(see p70)*, Sauce *(p37)* and Five Green *(p70)*.

*Bargaining is expected at the souqs; see p109 for tips*

### 7 Electronics/Digital Products

The range of electronic products is enormous – if there's a gadget on the market, you'll get it here. The tax-free environment means prices are low, but competition (don't be surprised to see a dozen electronics stores all in a row) means amazing prices and bargains if you shop around.

### 8 Global Designer Brands

Being tax-free, the world's best designers and exclusive labels here go for a fraction of the price they do elsewhere. ⊗ *Map P2 • Madinat Zayed neighbourhood, Abu Dhabi • Open 10am–1pm & 4–10pm Sat–Thu, 4pm–10pm Fri*

### 9 Arabic & Middle Eastern Music

You'll hear music everywhere in the Emirates, whether it's traditional songs performed at a heritage village, Egyptian pop on the radio, a Moroccan band in a restaurant or contemporary Arabic lounge at a hip bar. Buy Middle Eastern music at Virgin Megastore at the malls or at a music shop in the souqs.

### 10 Fun Souvenirs

Pick up some kitsch key rings and ashtrays, mosque-shaped alarm clocks, cuddly camels that play Arabic music when you squeeze them, or even Burj Al Arab paperweights.

**Humorous souvenirs**

## Top 10 Places to Buy Arabian Handicrafts & Souvenirs

### 1 Al Jaber Gallery
An Aladdin's cave selling exotic Arabian handicraft and souvenirs *(see p62)*.

### 2 Al Orooba Oriental
The finest carpets and kilims, along with antique prayer beads, silver jewellery and ceramics *(see p70)*.

### 3 Showcase Antiques Art and Frames
A collection of old Bedouin jewellery, khanjars and coffee pots. ⊗ *Map C2 • Jumeirah Rd, Umm Suqeim, Dubai • 04 348 8797 • Open 10am–1pm & 4–10pm Sat–Thu, 4–8pm Fri*

### 4 Pride of Kashmir
Renowned for soft pashmina shawls, carpets, cushions and throws *(see p62)*.

### 5 Gallery One Fine Art Photographs
Black and white photographs of Dubai's iconic symbols. ⊗ *Map C2 • Madinat Jumeirah, Dubai • 04 368 6055*

### 6 Khalifa Centre
Bargain for carpets and handicrafts here *(see p92)*.

### 7 Allah-din Shoes
Beautiful sequinned slippers. ⊗ *Map J1 • Bur Dubai Souq, Dubai, by the abra dock • 050 515 4351*

### 8 Camel Company
Shop for cute camel gifts. ⊗ *Map C2 • Madinat Jumeirah, Dubai • 04 368 6048*

### 9 Ajmal
Arabian attars and oils in ornate bottles *(see p62)*.

### 10 Bateel
Buy dates in a variety of beautifully-packaged gift boxes *(see p37)*.

 *Dubai Duty Free at Dubai Airport has a wonderful range of well-priced souvenirs if you forget something.*

Left **A lit-up Almaz by Momo** Centre **Live music at Tajine** Right **A taste of Persia at Shabestan**

# Middle Eastern Restaurants

## 1 Tajine
A vast wooden door leads you to a sumptuous cultural dining experience at Tajine (a Moroccan clay cooking pot) with live music, candlelight and an exotic decor. Mezze or harira soup for starters can be followed by kebabs, aromatic tagines and couscous dishes *(see p83)*.

## 2 Marrakech
The mosaic-tiled walls, soft lighting and graceful arches create a strong North African atmosphere, completed by live oud and Moroccan classics like couscous royale and tagine kofta. Ask to sit in one of the half-moon booths. ◎ *Map C5 • Shangri-La Hotel, Sheikh Zayed Road • 04 343 8888 • Open 1pm–3pm & 8pm–12:30am • DDDDD*

## 3 Shahrzad
You will be enchanted by Shahrzad's magical setting of fountains and oriental carpets, as well as by the fresh bread, Persian kebabs and rice dishes. ◎ *Map L1 • Hyatt Regency Hotel, Deira • 04 209 1200 • Open 12:30pm–3pm & 7:30pm–1am Sun–Fri • DDDD*

## 4 Shabestan
The exquisite classic Persian cuisine, spectacular creek views and superlative service will take you on a pleasant journey to ancient Persia. ◎ *Map K2 • Radisson SAS Hotel • 04 205 7333 • Open 12:15pm–3:15pm & 7:15pm–11:15pm • DDD*

## 5 Awtar
A late dinner here is a spectacle with a nightly performance by an exuberant bellydancer. Friendly Lebanese waiters add to the vibrant atmosphere. The mezze is excellent. ◎ *Map J6 • Grand Hyatt Dubai • 04 317 1234 • Open 12:30pm–3pm & 7:30pm–3am Sun–Fri • DDD*

## 6 Al Nafoorah
Don't judge Al Nafoorah by its staid atmosphere – the Lebanese food is fresh, delicious and generous. You'll find an extensive menu, with great desserts. ◎ *Map D6 • Emirates Towers, Sheikh Zayed Road • 04 319 8088 • Open 12:30pm–3pm & 8pm–midnight • DD*

## 7 Shoo Fee Ma Fee
Book a table outdoors on the terrace overlooking the waterways. The emphasis here is on authentic Moroccan cuisine, with pigeon pastilla, lamb and camel kofta on the menu. The upper terrace offers cocktails and shisha *(see p83)*.

**Moroccan setting at Shoo Fee Ma Fee**

**A mouth-watering Lebanese dish at Awtar**

### Almaz by Momo
Renowned restaurateur Mourad "Momo" Mazouz makes his first foray into Dubai's dining scene with this modish Moroccan establishment. Snack on mezze or enjoy Moroccan classics such as pigeon pastilla before checking out their sheesha salon. ⊗ *Map C2 • Mall of the Emirates • 04 409 8877 • Open 10am–midnight Sun–Thu, 10am–1:30am Fri, 10am–midnight Sat • No alcohol • DDD*

### Bastakiah Nights
With its rooftop overlooking historic Bastakiya, this is a gem of a restaurant offering unrivalled views of old Dubai. A must-visit for authentic Arabic and Emirati cuisine, seated at a low table overlooking the torch-lit court-yard or in an intimate indoor room *(see pp12–13)*.

### Al Tannour
To really soak up the ebullient Lebanese atmosphere, arrive fashionably late, preferably after 11pm, when the live music kicks off at this hugely popular haunt. You will need a lie-in the next day, but the food, friendly service and entertainment will have been memorable. ⊗ *Map E5 • Crowne Plaza Hotel, Sheikh Zayed Road • 04 331 1111 • Open 8:30pm–3am • DDDD; includes entertainment, but not alcohol*

## Top 10 Restaurants

**1 Verre**
A consistently high gastronomic treat *(see p63)*.

**2 Mezzanine**
Visit for British classics overseen by celebrity chef Gary Rhodes. ⊗ *Map B2 • Grosvenor House Dubai, Dubai Marina • 04 399 8888 • Open 11pm–3am • DDDDD*

**3 Eau Zone**
Pool-side setting and imaginative fusion cuisine. ⊗ *Map B2 • One&Only Royal Mirage, Al Sufouh • 04 399 9999 • Open 9am–1am • DDDDD*

**4 Fire & Ice**
Contemporary culinary fireworks and icy concoctions *(see p71)*.

**5 Nina**
Stylish venue attracting Bollywood starlets. Good for Indian cuisine with a modern twist *(see p83)*.

**6 La Baie**
Classic fine dining, with an emphasis on seafood and French cuisine. ⊗ *Map B1 • The Ritz-Carlton Jumeirah • 04 399 4000 • Open 10am–1pm & 4pm–10pm Sat–Thu, 4pm–10pm Fri • DDDDD*

**7 Bord Eau**
French classics and contemporary dishes at this chic restaurant *(see p93)*.

**8 Hoi An**
French-Vietnamese fusion cuisine served in a Far-Eastern atmosphere *(see p76)*.

**9 Zheng He's**
Superb Chinese delicacies served in style at an exquisite waterside location. The dim sum is delicious *(see p83)*.

**10 Peppercrab**
Sensational upmarket oriental seafood cuisine – try their signature dish *(see p71)*.

For a guide to restaurant prices, see p63.

Left **The stylish Bar 44** Centre **Sho Cho's wooden deck** Right **Moroccan-styled The Rooftop**

# Best Bars in Dubai

### 1 The Rooftop
It's easy to fall in love with the magical look and feel of this atmospheric Moroccan-style rooftop bar with its Arabesque lanterns and Oriental lounge music *(see p85)*.

### 2 Bahri Bar
You'll be impressed with the enchanting old-Arabian architecture and sumptuous interiors of Mina A'Salam hotel and its colonial-styled bar with verandas covered in Persian carpets. It also offers a mesmerizing view of the Burj Al Arab *(see p85)*.

### 3 Sho Cho's
There is no more sublime spot for a drink than on Sho Cho's wooden deck by the beach. Low-key early in the evening when people head here for the sushi, Dubai's style-setters pack the place late for excellent DJs *(see p85)*.

### 4 The Agency
These stylish wine bars attract a sophisticated set who are serious about their wine. The Jumeirah Emirates Towers branch is just right for a quick drink and tasty "wine teasers" (tapas-style snacks); Madinat Jumeirah is perfect for a relaxed night out *(see p85)*.

### 5 Buddha Bar
You'll want to linger at this atmospheric bar, which attracts a fashionable crowd of regulars

**A beautifully lit Lotus One**

who flock here for the Oriental decor, Asian tapas and exotic cocktails. This one is better than its more touristy Paris parent. Expect to see some dancing on the tables *(see p85)*.

### 6 1897
This stylish cocktail bar is named after the year Kempinski Hotels were founded. Sink into a purple velvet sofa and enjoy some of the best cocktails in Dubai, along with smooth jazz sounds. ⊗ *Map C2 • Kempinski Mall of the Emirates Hotel, Dubai • 04 341 0000 • Open noon–2am*

### 7 Lotus One
This is the city's most beautifully lit bar, with fibre-optic lighting, filmy curtains, swinging seats and sand under the glass floor. It attracts big name DJs, such as Pierre Raven. After working up an appetite on the dance floor, try the tasty Asian-inspired tapas. The regulars are as beautiful as the bar *(see p77)*.

*Dubai's resident expats hit the city's bars around 6pm for sunset or after 10pm for post-dinner drinks.*

### The Terrace

**8** Reclining on one of the low sofas listening to the water lapping at the boats on Dubai Creek is about as relaxing as it can get. Add some oysters, champagne and caviar (the house specialities) to the equation and you're bound to have a sublime experience. Vodka lovers will be pleased – the Terrace prides itself on its extensive vodka menu *(see p65)*.

### Bar 44

**9** Prop yourself up at the swanky circular bar or sink into a plush chair at this swish cocktail bar on level 44 (hence the name) of the Grosvenor House hotel with spectacular views over Dubai Marina. It attracts a regular sophisticated local set as well as visiting business people out to impress colleagues *(see p85)*.

### Tamanya Terrace

**10** This alfresco terrace on top of one of Dubai's chicest hotels has spectacular views over Dubai Media City and the towers of Dubai Marina. Head here at sunset for a sheesha and cocktail or come late for a dance when nights such as "Favela Chic" attract a lively Latino crowd.
Ⓢ *Map B2 • Radisson SAS Hotel Dubai Media City, Al Sufouh Rd, Jumeirah • 04 366 9111 • Open 5pm–2am*

**Cocktails at Tamanya Terrace**

## Top 10 Sheesha Spots

**1 Sheesha Courtyard**
Relax in a shady cushion-strewn courtyard. Ⓢ *Map B2 • One&Only Royal Mirage Hotel, Jumeirah, Dubai • 04 399 9999 • Open 7pm–late*

**2 Kan Zaman**
A smoke under the stars. Ⓢ *Map K1 • Heritage & Diving Village, Shindagha, Dubai • 04 393 9913 • Open 11pm–3am*

**3 Cosmo**
Indulge in people-watching here. Ⓢ *Map D6 • The Tower, Sheikh Zayed Rd, Dubai • 04 332 6569 • Open 9am–1am*

**4 Shakespeare's**
Popular French Baroque-style patisserie. Ⓢ *Map D4 • The Village Mall, Jumeirah Beach Rd, Jumeirah, Dubai • 04 331 1757 • Open 8am–1am*

**5 Souq Madinat Jumeirah Plaza**
A breezy, magical sheesha-smoking spot *(see pp18–19)*.

**6 QDs**
An expat favourite overlooking the Creek *(see p65)*.

**7 Zari Zardozi**
Soak up the exotic Indian atmosphere *(see p93)*.

**8 Al Areesh**
A palm-frond summer house on the waterfront. Ⓢ *Map K1 • Heritage & Diving Village, Shindagha, Dubai, and the Mina (port), Abu Dhabi • 04 368 6048 • Open 5pm–1am*

**9 Al Hakawati Café**
Smoke amongst towering skyscrapers. Ⓢ *Map B2 • Dubai Marina, Jumeirah, Dubai • 04 343 3128 • Open 10am–1am*

**10 Special Sheesha Café**
Join the locals at these simple cafés. Ⓢ *Several branches in the parks on the Abu Dhabi Corniche • Open 24 hours*

*Smoking flavoured tobacco from a sheesha pipe, also known as a hubbly bubbly or hooka pipe, is a popular Emirati pastime.*

Left **The Jumeirah Beach Hotel** Centre **Mina A'Salam's beach** Right **Pool at Mina Seyahi Resort**

# 🔟 Beach Resorts

### 1 One&Only Royal Mirage

This luxury resort oozes old-fashioned Moroccan romance. Built in truly regal style, it sits on its own sandy beach, amidst acres of landscaped gardens filled with beautiful palm-fringed pools, gushing fountains and candlelit walkways. Explore this divine escape's three intimate properties: The Palace, the Arabian Court and the Residence & Spa. ◈ *Map B1 • Al Sufouh Rd, Jumeirah, Dubai • 04 399 9999 • www.oneandonlyresorts.com • DDDDD*

### 2 Mina A'Salam

For a room with a view, this magical kasbah-inspired hotel, part of the vast Arabian-style Madinat Jumeirah, will not disappoint. It is built overlooking an enchanting harbour around which much of the hotel experience is based. Relax in your room's sea-facing balcony, which opens onto the soft sand beach or chill on the extensive terraces of its many restaurants, bars and lounges *(see pp18–19)*.

**A beach pavilion at One&Only Royal Mirage**

### 3 Al Qasr

Designed in the style of a mythical Arabian palace, this magnificent hotel has deluxe rooms and suites. Surrounded by water, it forms a virtual island that offers you a view of ancient windtowers, pools, meandering waterways and the pristine white sand beach *(see pp18-19)*.

### 4 Jumeirah Beach Hotel

Set on the shores of the Arabian Gulf and built in a startling shape that mirrors a breaking wave, this landmark 600-room hotel has its own beach and six swimming pools. If you are feeling adventurous, try the adjacent Wild Wadi Water Park, to which guests have unlimited access. ◈ *Map C1 • Jumeirah Beach Rd, Jumeirah, Dubai • 04 348 0000 • www.jumeirahbeach-hotel.com • DDDDD*

### 5 Le Royal Meridien Beach Resort & Spa

One of the Meridien's flagship hotels, this opulent property comprises the main hotel and Tower and Club complexes, all with sea-facing rooms. You'll love the landscaped gardens, spa and temperature-controlled pools. ◈ *Map B1 • Al Sofouh Rd, Jumeirah, Dubai • 04 399 5555 • www.leroyalmeridien-dubai.com • DDDDD*

### 6 Le Meridien Mina Seyahi Resort

If you love outdoor pursuits, this relaxed resort is just right for

**The luxurious pool at Le Royal Meridien Beach Resort & Spa**

you. Indulge in a variety of activities, including tennis, sailing, wind-surfing and deep-sea fishing. ◈ *Map B1 • Al Sufouh Rd, Jumeirah, Dubai • 04 399 3333 • www. lemeridien-minaseyahi.com • DDDDD*

### Ritz Carlton
With Mediterranean architecture, tropical gardens leading to a golden beach and just 138 guest rooms, this hotel promises exclusivity. Especially good for couples with made-for-two sun loungers, an adults-only pool, a Balinese spa and classy sunset bars and restaurants. ◈ *Map B1 • Al Sufouh Rd, Jumeirah, Dubai • 04 399 4000 • www.ritzcarlton. com • DDDDD*

### Hilton Dubai Jumeirah
If it's a beach holiday you are after, this 400-room family-focussed resort offers comfortable rooms with balconies, a white sandy beach and a massive pool with a swim-up bar. Try the in-house restaurant, BiCE *(see p83)*, for some fine Italian food. ◈ *Map B1 • Al Sufouh Rd, Jumeirah, Dubai • 04 399 1111 • www.hilton.com • DDDDD*

### Habtoor Grand Resort & Spa
This shiny 446-room modern resort opened in 2005 on the seafront, close to Dubai Marina. Guest rooms are located within two high towers, all with garden or sea views. The hotel has its own private beach, three swimming pools, a spa, a health club, restaurants, squash and tennis courts, a children's club and a beach water sports centre. Make sure you visit the stunning infinity pool on the mezzanine between the towers. ◈ *Map B1 • Al Sufouh Rd, Jumeirah, Dubai • 04 399 5000 • www.grandjumeirah. habtoorhotels.com • DDDDD*

### Jumeirah Beach Club & Spa
This very exclusive boutique resort has an intimate ambience. Its excellent facilities are set in the lushest of gardens overlooking the azure waters of the Gulf. Recently refurbished as an all-suite hotel with Polynesian suites and water bungalows, it remains a haven of tranquillity. ◈ *Map A4 • Jumeirah Beach Rd, Jumeirah, Dubai • 04 344 5333 • www. jumeirahbeachclub.com • DDDDD*

Left **The Givenchy Spa** Right **Senso, Wellness Centre**

# TOP 10 Spas

### 1 Assawan Spa
The infinity pool in this stunning spa with its lavish ancient Middle Eastern decor, 18 floors up above the Arabian Gulf, says it all: pure luxury, with its long views of sea and sky. Visit for exotic massages and wraps *(see pp16–17)*.

### 2 Givenchy Spa
A Moroccan hammam with heated marble tables under soaring domes is a signature feature of this understated spa. It has 12 luxury treatment rooms. ⊗ *Map B2 • One&Only Royal Mirage, Dubai • 04 315 2140 • www.oneandonlyresort.com*

### 3 Talise Spa
Arrive by *abra* along waterways to the 26 treatment rooms, including sunken, wet, colour, crystal and light therapy rooms. There is a 25-minute consultation session before the treatment – the choice here is extensive. ⊗ *Map C2 • Madinat Jumeirah, Dubai • 04 366 6818 • www.madinatjumeirah.com*

### 4 Softouch Spa
This spa uses Ayurvedic healing combined with a range of modern techniques to combat the stress and strain of modern lifestyles. ⊗ *Map C2 • Kempinski Mall of the Emirates Hotel • 04 341 0000 • www.kempinski-dubai.com*

**An objet d'art at the Softouch Spa**

### 5 Willow Stream Spa
This is a Greco-Roman themed spa with terrace sun-decks and a unique Middle Eastern feel to the treatments. ⊗ *Map E5 • Fairmont Hotel, Sheikh Zayed Rd, Dubai • 04 332 5555 • www.willowstream.com*

### 6 Cleopatra's Spa
The spirit of ancient Egypt infuses this spa. Some original treatments include O-Lys light therapy and exotic lime and ginger exfoliation. ⊗ *Map H5 • Wafi City, Dubai • 04 324 7700 • www.waficity.com*

### 7 Male Spa at The Pyramids
The Male Spa has earned a reputation for its deep tissue massages and detox wraps for men. The 72-jet strong hydrobath is an invigorating way to unwind. ⊗ *Map H5 • Wafi City, Dubai • 04 324 7700 • www.waficity.com*

**The serene decor at Willow Stream**

*For a luxurious day of pampering, be sure to phone ahead and reserve a place. Ask if any promotional packages are available.*

**Egyptian-themed Cleopatra's Spa**

### 8 Senso, Wellness Centre

A contemporary urban spa located in the heart of Dubai Media City with five differently themed treatment rooms. Choose from a vast selection of therapies guaranteed to chase the stress away. ⊗ *Map B2 • The Radisson SAS Hotel, Dubai Media City, Dubai • 04 366 9111 • www.radissonsas.com*

### 9 Eden Spa & Health Club

Soothing daylight and the sound of rippling water create an air of serenity here. The "aqua-medic" pools are filled with mineral-rich waters and situated under a glass-domed ceiling. Treatments include massage, aromatherapy, wraps and mineral baths. There's also a Turkish hammam here. ⊗ *Map P1 • Le Meridien, Abu Dhabi • 02 644 6666*

### 10 Hiltonia Spa

There are five treatment rooms at this very professionally managed spa. Spa users can enjoy the eucalyptus steam room, cold plunge shower, sauna and whirlpool overlooking the resort's own beach and swimming pools. ⊗ *Map P6 • Hilton Hotel, Abu Dhabi • 02 692 4336*

## Top 10 Spa Treatments

### 1 Canyon Love Stone Therapy

A 75-minute massage using warm and cold volcanic stones. ⊗ *Givenchy Spa*

### 2 Frangipani Body Nourish Wrap

Tahitian coconut and frangipani flowers are used to give a glow. ⊗ *Cleopatra's Spa*

### 3 Caviar Body Treatment

A whole-body massage using La Prairie caviar-based products. ⊗ *Assawan*

### 4 Fingerprint Massage

As the name suggests, this massage is uniquely personalized by your therapist after a personal consultation. ⊗ *Talise Spa*

### 5 Ayurveda Massage

A head-to-toe massage by two therapists using synchronous rhythm. ⊗ *Softouch Spa*

### 6 Essence of Moroccan Rose Oil

A treatment of exfoliation followed by a Moroccan rose oil massage. ⊗ *Willow Stream*

### 7 Body Mask

An anti-aging massage and body mask using Ingrid Millet products. ⊗ *Senso*

### 8 Blueberry and Blackberry Facial

A delicious cocktail of natural fruit extracts to hydrate and rejuvenate. ⊗ *Hiltonia Spa*

### 9 Sea Tonic Firming Treatment, Eden Spa

A revitalising body massage and facial treatment using French-derived phytomer. ⊗ *Eden Spa*

### 10 Elemis IQ Facial

A performance-enhancing deep cleansing facial that helps to eliminate blocked pores. ⊗ *Male Spa*

*Many hotel packages combine several treatments with use of the hotel pool and leisure facilities.*

Left **Lift stop at Ski Dubai** Centre **Encounter Zone at Wafi Mall** Right **Children's City**

# Activities for Kids

### Wild Wadi Water Park
Dare to try the 30 adrenalin-fuelled watery rides or just float about on a rubber ring along the waterways here *(see pp78–81)*.

### Ski Dubai Snow Park
Go skiing or snow-boarding on the slopes of this icy dome *(see p32)*. ❄ Map C2 • Mall of the Emirates, Dubai • 04 409 4000 • Open 10am–11pm Sun–Wed, 10am–midnight Thu–Sat • Adm • www.skidxb.com

### Dubai Museum
The clever reconstructions will ensure that you enjoy the experience of an Arabian souq's aroma of spices or the sounds of an old school *(see pp8–9)*.

### Stargate
Kids will love the 3D games, space maze, 3-D theatre and IMAX cinema. ❄ Map F6 • Za'abeel Park, Dubai • 04 398 6888 • Adm

### Children's City
Zoom off on a space ride at the planetarium or explore the human body at the discovery centre. There's a nature centre and a toddler area too. ❄ Map J6 • Creekside Park, Dubai • 04 336 7633 • Open 9am–8:30pm Sat–Thu, 3pm–8:30pm Fri • Adm • www.childrencity.ae

### Magic Planet
There's everything from a merry-go-round, bumper cars, pitch and putt and video games for children to a soft-play area for toddlers, to ensure that you can shop in peace! ❄ Map L5 • Deira City Centre (see p62)• 04 295 1010 • Adm for rides • www.deiracity.com

### Ibn Battuta Mall Storytelling Tour
Another opportunity for kids to be entertained while you shop! Costumed storytellers lead interesting tours in the footsteps

**The Wild Wadi's water delights**

*The admission fee for Ski Dubai Snow Park includes hire of all the necessary equipment for children.*

**The fun-filled Za'abeel Park**

of famed Arabian explorer, Ibn Battuta. ✆ Map A2 • Ibn Battuta Mall, Dubai • 04 362 1900 • Open 9:30am–1:30pm & 4:30pm–8:30pm Sat–Thu • www.ibnbattutamall.com

### 8 WonderLand Theme & Water Park

Have a fun-filled day enjoying the activity pools, skate park, rides and food outlets. ✆ Map J6 • Creekside Park, Dubai • 04 324 1222 • Open 2pm–10pm Sat–Wed, noon–11pm Thu–Fri • Adm • www.wonderlanduae.com

### 9 Dubai Desert Extreme Skate Park

Adventurous kids will love the half-pipes, trick boxes, rail slides and mini-ramps for BMX-ers, skateboarders and inline skaters. All equipment can be hired; helmets are compulsory. ✆ Map J6 • Creekside Park, Dubai • 04 324 1222 • Open 2pm–10pm Sat–Wed, noon–11pm Thu–Fri • Adm

### 10 Encounter Zone

Another shop and drop deal for kids. Lunarland is for under-8s, with a snow capsule, gentle rollercoaster and Skylab tunnels. Older kids can try the Galactica's Crystal Maze (a challenging mental game), the anti-gravity racing simulator and 3D cinema. ✆ Map H5 • Wafi Shopping Mall, Dubai • 04 324 7747 • Open 10am–10pm Sat-Tue, 10am–11pm Wed–Thu, 1pm–10pm Fri • Adm

## Top 10 Parks, Gardens & Beaches

**1 Creekside Park**
A huge botanical park with BBQ areas, mini golf course and cable car (see pp10–11).

**2 Za'abeel Park**
Technology themed park with football field, boating lake and cafés (see pp72–75).

**3 Al Seef Rd Park**
A great place to enjoy the Creek action. ✆ Map K2 • Dubai

**4 Jumeirah Beach Park**
Landscaped play areas and a beach with showers and sunbeds (see pp78–81).

**5 Al Mamzar Beach Park**
Enjoy the huge picnic areas and four swimming beaches by hired bike or the park mini train. ✆ Map F1 • Al Hamriya, Dubai • 971 4 296 6201 • Open 8am–10pm • Adm • Wed is for women and children only

**6 Umm Suqeim Beach**
Public beach with shallow waters and great views of the Burj Al Arab. ✆ Map C2 • Off Jumeirah Beach Road, Dubai

**7 Safa Park**
A huge park with lots to do. Try the trampoline cage for fun (see pp78–81).

**8 Mushrif Park**
A desert park with pools, an enclosure with farm animals and a miniature house exhibit. ✆ Dubai • Open 8am–10:30pm Sat–Wed, 8am–11:30pm Thu–Fri • Adm

**9 Russian Beach**
This lively local beach is popular with Russian expats and tourists (see pp78–81).

**10 Kite Beach**
Popular for kite surfing and parasailing. ✆ Map C2 • Umm Suqeim, behind Wollongong University, Dubai

Left **Wind surfing** Right **Pro-karts at the Dubai Autodrome**

# 🔟 Outdoor Activities

### 1 Scuba Diving
A popular local activity, you will find good diving in Dubai, Abu Dhabi and some of the East Coast towns. 🔊 *Map K1 • Emirates Diving Association, Heritage and Diving Villages, Shindagha, has information on diving in the UAE • 04 393 9390 • www.emiratesdiving.com*

### 2 Fishing
Join an organized fishing trip where equipment is provided. Cook your fish on board or even charter your own boat. 🔊 *Map B2 & Q1 • Le Meridien Mina Seyahi Resort, Dubai (see p44); Marina Beach Rotana Hotel & Towers, Abu Dhabi (see p116)*

### 3 Kite Surfing
Join the friendly local kite surfers on Dubai's popular Kite Beach. You can hire or buy equipment from North Kites, who can help connect you with instructors. 🔊 *Map C1 • Kite Beach, Jumeirah Beach Rd, Jumeirah Beach, Dubai • Arabian Gulf Kite Club: 050 455 5216; North Kites: 04 394 1258 • www.dubaikiteclub.com*

### 4 Wind Surfing
Great winds make Dubai ideal for wind surfing. Most good beach resorts hire out wind-surfing equipment and also offer windsurfing lessons. 🔊 *Map B1 • Le Royal Meridien Beach Resort (see p44)*

### 5 Sailing
The Gulf winds are great for sailing. Hire a catamaran if you are an experienced sailor.

Beginners can take lessons. 🔊 *Map B2 • Le Meridien Mina Seyahi Resort & Marina, Dubai (see p44); Abu Dhabi International Sailing School, Abu Dhabi Marina: 02 681 3446*

### 6 Skateboarding
While there's lots of concrete to please adventurous street skaters, you can rent skateboards and helmets (compulsory) from Dubai Desert Extreme and ride the massive half-pipe at Dubai's Creekside Park *(see pp10–11).* 🔊 *Map J6 • www.dubaidesertextreme.com • Adm*

### 7 Hot-air Ballooning
Getting a bird's-eye-view from a hot air balloon is simply sublime. Only by floating way above the dunes can you fully appreciate the waves of sand and patterns of light and shadow

**A hot-air balloon set to take off**

**A wakeboarder in action**

crafted by the ridges that are impossible to see from the ground. ✆ *Dubai • 04 273 8585 • Oct–May • www.ballooning.ae*

### Wakeboarding
Try your hand at some wakeboarding tricks as you ride the waves on the Arabian Gulf sea. Ask your resort for a trainer if you're a first-timer. ✆ *Map B2 & P6 • Le Meridien Mina Seyahi Resort & Marina, Dubai (see p44); Hiltonia Beach Club, Abu Dhabi: 02 692 4205, www.hilton.com*

### Horseriding
Where better to mount a horse than in the Middle East's undisputed equestrian capital? Indulge in a bit of horseriding in Dubai or even polo in Abu Dhabi. ✆ *Map D3 • Dubai Equestrian Centre, by Nad Al Sheba Racecourse (see pp72–5); Abu Dhabi Equestrian Club: 02 445 5500*

### Motor Racing
Adrenaline-junkies can burn rubber driving pro-karts at the Dubai Autodrome. The Formula One standard racing circuit has 17 hair-raising turns! Book ahead for lessons at the driving school. ✆ *Dubai Autodrome Kart-drome, Emirates Rd, Dubai • 04 367 8700 • www. dubaiautodrome.com*

## Top 10 Golf Courses

### Emirates Golf Club
The famous Dubai Desert Classic is held here *(see p53)*. ✆ *Map B2 • 04 380 2222 • www.dubaigolf.com*

### The Montgomerie
A splendid course with sprawling, undulating lawns. ✆ *Map B2 • 04 390 5600 • www.themontgomerie.com*

### Dubai Creek Golf & Yacht Club
One of the world's best, by the Creekside *(see pp58–61)*.

### The Desert Course
Challenging lush fairways through desert sands. ✆ *Map B3 • 04 366 3000 • www. arabianranchesgolfdubai.com*

### Nad Al Sheba Club
A Scottish-style 18-hole course *(see p74)*.

### Dubai Sports City
Look out for the Ernie Els designed golf course opening late 2007. ✆ *Map C3 • Dubailand • www.dubaisportscity.com*

### Four Seasons Al Badia Golf Club
A superb Robert Trent Jones II-designed course. ✆ *Map E3 • 04 285 5772 • www. albadiagolfresort.com*

### The Resort Course
Enjoy Arabian Gulf vistas as you tee off with the peacocks. ✆ *04 804 8058 • www. jebelali-international.com*

### Al Ghazal Golf Club
A full-sand course with top-class teaching technology. ✆ *Near Abu Dhabi International Airport • 02 575 8040*

### Abu Dhabi Golf Club
Golfers love this serene 18-hole course. It features on the European Tour list. ✆ *Map N2 • 02 558 8990 • www. adgolfsheraton.com*

Left **Locals and expats queuing at a cinema** Right **The Hyatt Galleria ice rink**

# 🔟 Indoor Activities

### Snow Sports
What better place to escape the scorching heat than on the slopes of Ski Dubai. You can have skiing lessons, practice snow-boarding tricks or take the kids on a toboggan ride in the children's snow park *(see p32)*.

### Ice-skating
The cities' ice rinks are ideal for cooling off while taking in a bit of local colour. Europeans head to the rinks when they get homesick in winter. ⬥ *Map L1 • Abu Dhabi Ice-Skating Rink, Abu Dhabi; Hyatt Galleria, Hyatt Regency Hotel, Dubai • AD Ice-Skating Rink: 02 449 2271; Hyatt Regency Hotel: 04 317 2222, 209 1234 • Open 8am–10pm • Adm*

### Movie-going
You're likely to see films from India, the Arab world and the Philippines screening along-side Hollywood blockbusters. ⬥ *Map L5 & N5 • Cinestar Deira City Centre mall, Dubai; Cinestar Marina Mall, Abu Dhabi • Cinestar Deira: 04 294 9000; Cinestar Abu Dhabi: 02 681 8484 • Open 11am–late • Adm*

### Fencing
Fancy a bout of fencing or just a look inside the magnificent Madinat Jumeirah health club? Join the Dubai Fencing Club for a spot of jousting. ⬥ *Map C2 • Dubai Fencing Club, Madinat Jumeirah, Dubai • 04 366 8888, 050 7944 190 • See website for schedule • Adm; all equipment included in price • www. dubaifencingclub.com*

**Indoor rock climbing**

### Rock Climbing
Try your hand at scaling the UAE's only state-of-the-art 15 m (50 ft) high indoor climbing wall. ⬥ *Map H5 • Pharaoh's Club, Pyramids, Wafi City, Dubai • 04 324 7700 • Adm • www.waficity.com*

### Shooting
See how good your aim is in one of ten hi-tech pistol-shooting lanes at the Cinetronic Firearms Simulator Room, or try your hand at clay shooting on outdoor ranges at the Jebel Ali Shooting Club. ⬥ *Map A2 • Jebel Ali Shooting Club, Jebel Ali, Dubai • 04 883 6555 • Open 1pm–9pm Mon–Wed • Adm*

### Bowling
There's nothing an Emirati loves more than following bowls with some sheesha. The lanes of choice are at Dubai's oldest bowling alley, Thunderbowl,

*Participating in and watching sporting events is a great way to get to know the locals.*

where they can puff outside afterwards overlooking busy Sheikh Zayed Rd. Expats prefer Al Nasr Leisureland. ◈ *Map C6 & H4 • Thunderbowl, Sheikh Zayed Rd, Interchange 1, Dubai; Al Nasr Leisureland, behind American Hospital, Oud Metha, Dubai • Thunderbowl: 04 343 1000; Leisureland: 04 3337 1234 • Open 9am–midnight • Adm; includes shoes*

**8** **Ice Hockey**
The Abu Dhabi Falcons meet on weekday evenings at the huge Abu Dhabi ice rink and are more than happy for you to join in or cheer them on. ◈ *Abu Dhabi Ice Rink, off Airport Rd, behind Carrefour • 02 444 8458 • Adm*

**9** **Belly Dancing**
Join Abu Dhabi's expat women for a lesson or two in how to shimmy like the best of them. ◈ *Map N1 • Sheraton Abu Dhabi Resort & Towers, Abu Dhabi (see p116) • Sun & Tue • Adm*

**10** **Billiards, Snooker & Pool**
Hear tales of local life over a friendly game of billiards, snooker or pool. You can also have a game of darts and a lager at an English style pub. ◈ *Map P1 • Rock Bottom Café, Abu Dhabi (see p96); Aussie Legends, Dubai • Aussie Legends: 04 398 2222 • Adm*

**A game of ice hockey**

## Top 10 Spectator Sports & Events

**1** **Dubai World Cup**
Dress up for the world's richest horse race with a $6 million prize (see p35).

**2** **Dubai Desert Classic**
Watch the world's best golfers compete in this 4-day tournament (see p35).

**3** **Dubai Tennis Championships**
See the big guns of world tennis serve action at Dubai Tennis Stadium (see p35).

**4** **Dubai Rugby Sevens**
The first leg of the Sevens World Tour, this big excuse for a beer fest is loved by rugby fans the world over. ◈ *Nov • www.dubairugby7s.com*

**5** **Camel Racing**
Watch Emiratis drive their 4WDs around the track beside their camels. ◈ *Al Wathba Camel Track, 45 km east of Abu Dhabi • Oct–Mar Thu–Fri*

**6** **A1 Grand Prix**
This open-wheeled auto racing series has a round in Dubai. ◈ *www.a1gp.com*

**7** **UAE Football**
The fans' choreographed dances and songs are just as riveting as the play on the field. ◈ *Winter weekday nights • www.uaefootball.org*

**8** **Powerboat Racing**
Watch the lightweight catamarans in exciting action. ◈ *Dec • www.f1boat.com*

**9** **Dubai Marathon**
Runners from all around the world compete on the city streets (see p35).

**10** **Desert Challenge**
Bikes, 4WDs and even trucks take part in this international cross country rally through the desert (see p35).

*Coincide your visit to the UAE with a major event to see the cities at their best.*

Left **Al Ain Palace Museum** Centre **Hatta's Heritage Village** Right **Liwa's sandswept roads**

# 10 Excursions

### 1 Sharjah

The Sharjah Art Museum, the Heritage Museum and the Archaeological Museum are a must visit. The souqs are good for shopping. ✆ *10 km from Dubai*
• *Sharjah Art Museum: 06 568 8222*
• *Heritage Museum: 06 569 3999*
• *Archaeological Museum: 06 566 5466*

### 2 Al Ain

Known as Garden City, this green emirate is home to the Al Ain Palace Museum. Also here are the Al Ain Livestock Souq and the Jahili Fort. ✆ *160 km from Dubai*
• *Al Ain Palace Museum: 03 715 7755*
• *Jahili Fort: next to Al Ain Rotana Hotel •*
*Al Ain Camel Souq: Al Ain-Buraimi border*

### 3 Hatta

Visit the Heritage Village at this serene oasis town. A drive into the mountains leads to the clear Hatta Rock Pools. ✆ *105 km from Dubai • Heritage Village: Open 8am– 7:30pm Sat–Thu, 3pm–9pm Fri*

### 4 Fujairah

Fujairah has a coastline of coral reefs and hillsides with forts and watchtowers. The Fujairah Fort is the oldest in the UAE, dating to 1670. Watch a bit of bloodless bull butting on a Friday here. ✆ *130 km from Dubai*

### 5 Khor Kalba

This small fishing village has the oldest mangrove in Arabia and is now a conservation area. Explore its swamps by canoe.
✆ *10 km south of Fujairah • Canoeing: Desert Rangers: www.desertrangers.com*

### 6 Bidiya

This tiny fishing village is home to the oldest mosque in the UAE, dating back to 1446. Made from mud brick, stone and gypsum, it is now restored with its four small domes held up by a massive central pillar. ✆ *38 km north of Fujairah • Visit outside of prayer times, accompanied by a mosque guide*

**The Blue Souq at Sharjah**

**A dhow trip at Musandam Peninsula**

### Khor Fakkan
A pretty coastal town that sits on a curving bay, this makes a good draw for divers, thanks to the excellent visibility and reef potential. ◈ *15 km north of Fujairah • Khor Fakkan Dive Centre: 09 237 0299*

### Dibba
A sleepy spot with an open beach. Nearby is Sandy Beach, with one of the best dive centres in the area and close to an ocean outcrop called Snoopy Island – ideal for snorkelling and diving. Sandy Beach Motel is a lovely lunch spot. ◈ *130 km from Dubai • Sandy Beach Motel: 09 244 5555 • Sandy Beach Diving Centre: 09 244 5555*

### Musandam Peninsula
Boasting spectacular mountain cliffs and a coastline of inlets and fjords, this northerly enclave is part of Oman. Visit to enjoy day-long *dhow* trips into the fjords, snorkel and see dolphins. ◈ *193 km from Dubai • Khasab Travel & Tours: www.khasabtours. com • Visa available at Oman entry point*

### Liwa
Liwa's high golden dunes, some hundreds of metres high, are almost devoid of vegetation yet close by are flourishing date-producing farms – an awesome spectacle. ◈ *300 km from Abu Dhabi*

## Top 10 Tours

**1 Arabian Adventures**
Enjoy city tours, desert safaris, dune bashing, camel riding, sand skiing and more. ◈ *www.arabian-adventures.com*

**2 Net Tours**
Reliable city tours, desert safaris, mountain tours, *dhow* cruises plus trips to Oman. ◈ *www.nettoursdubai.com*

**3 Bateaux Dubai Cruises**
Lunchtime sight-seeing and gourmet dinner cruises down Dubai Creek. ◈ *www. jebelali-international.com*

**4 Danat Dubai**
Try an Afternoon Sundowner cruise with this *dhow* operator. ◈ *www. danatdubaicruises.com*

**5 Creekside Leisure**
Recline in a cushioned majlis and watch the sun set aboard a *dhow* on the Creek. ◈ *www.tour-dubai.com*

**6 Nad Al Sheba Club Tour**
Visit the world-class racehorse training facilities at the venue for Dubai World Cup *(see p74)*.

**7 Arabian Divers & Sportsfishing Charters**
Sport fishing in the Arabian Gulf off Abu Dhabi – try to spot dolphins and whales. ◈ *www.fishabudhabi.com*

**8 Big Bus Tour Company**
Hop aboard an open-air double-decker London bus around Dubai. ◈ *www.bigbus. co.uk/dub/html/dub_home.html*

**9 Wonder Bus Tours**
An amphibious 2-hour bus tour that starts on dry land and cruises on Dubai Creek. ◈ *www.wonderbusdubai.com*

**10 Orient Tours**
Ideal for 4WD tours to Al Ain, Liwa or the Mussandam. ◈ *www.orient-tours-uae.com*

# AROUND TOWN

DUBAI & ABU DHABI'S TOP 10

Left *Dhows* moored at the wharf Right The stunning Dubai Creek Golf & Yacht Club

# Around Dubai – Deira

THE TERM DEIRA IS USED TO DESCRIBE *the bustling commercial area north of the Creek. Deira is the source of Dubai's trading roots and it is around the Creek that you really get a sense of this. There is a telling contrast between the sight of the old wooden dhows moored at the wharfside reflected in the glass façades of the spectacularly sleek skyscrapers. Much of the dhow cargo is destined for the souqs and shopping districts of buzzy Deira. As a result, this area boasts some of Dubai's most atmospheric souq-life, especially at the Gold Souq, Spice Souq and Deira Souq. A major preservation effort by Dubai Municipality means that this area offers some architectural gems like the Al-Ahmadiya School and the Heritage House. The narrow streets and the general traffic congestion in the area mean that to enjoy it all, it's really best to explore on foot.*

A door at Heritage House

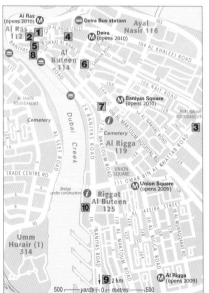

## Sights

1. Al-Ahmadiya School
2. Heritage House
3. Watchtower
4. Gold Souq
5. Spice Souq
6. Deira Souq
7. Baniyas Square
8. Dhow Wharfs
9. Dubai Creek Golf & Yacht Club
10. National Bank of Dubai

---

58  *Previous pages* **The stunning Jumeirah Mosque at dusk**

**The Al-Ahmadiya School**

### Al-Ahmadiya School

Dubai's first school, opened in 1912, was founded by a philanthropist pearl merchant. Maths, the Holy Koran and Arabic calligraphy were taught. The boys sat on palm mats. Many such schools were located in Emirati coastal cities with the support of leading merchants and Sheikhs, who subsidised the education. This school closed in 1963. Now a museum and worth visiting for its sheer architectural grace, it offers an educational insight into the past. ◈ *Map K1 • Al Khor St • 04 226 0286 • Open 8am–7:30pm Sat–Thu, 2:30pm–7:30pm Fri*

### Heritage House

This beautifully restored airy courtyard house dates back to the 1890s. Unusually, this 10-room building does not have a windtower, but the upper floor is designed with open doors and windows to draw in the Creek breezes. Now a museum giving an insight into Emirati life, you can explore the different rooms, all furnished to period, with dioramas. There are touchscreens too. ◈ *Map K1 • Al Khor St • 04 226 0286 • Open 7:30am–2:30pm Sat–Wed, 2pm–5pm Fri*

### Watchtower

Tucked away in the busy streets of Deira is a surprise: a beautifully restored mud-brick watchtower that stands in its own gardens. This round tower is Burj Nahar. It dates back to 1870 when it was one of three towers that served as part of Dubai's network of defences. Guards would scale the tower and keep watch for invaders during tribal disputes. The short masonry columns projecting above the roof level once held a palm frond *(barasti)* roof. ◈ *Map M2 • Omar Bin Al Khattab Rd*

### Gold Souq

You are unlikely to have ever seen so much gleaming gold as in Dubai's historic Gold Souq. The souq is still dominated by Indian and Iranian craftsmen and traders, as it has been for close on a century. It has been restored with a traditional Arabic arcade with arching wooden roof. You'll find jewellery in both Arabic and western styles *(see p20)*.

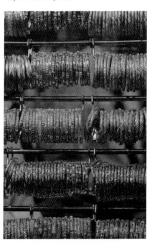

**Gold displays at Deira Gold Souq**

**Exotic spices at the Spice Souq**

### Spice Souq

Moody and atmospheric, the Spice Souq is a sensory trip into the past, where you can wander through a maze of narrow alleyways lined with shops piled high with aromatic spices. You'll find sacks of cinnamon sticks, frankincense, cumin, coriander seed and oud. Some great souvenir buys include frankincense (sold with charcoal burner), henna kits (for hand and body decoration), saffron and fragrant rose water *(see p20)*.

### Deira Souq

This is where you get a real taste of the melting pot of cultures that is Dubai. This souq is frequented by Emiratis and expats. The shops sell everything from bright Indian clothing to colourful kitchenware to electric household appliances to pirated CDs. It's a fascinating area to wander in. If you do plan to shop, remember, nothing is sold without haggling *(see p20)*.

### Deira History

Liberal trade policies are the roots of Deira which, by the early 20th century, had developed the largest souq on the Arabian coast. It became a natural haven for merchants who left Lingah, on the Persian coast, after the introduction of high customs there in 1902. They continued to trade with Lingah, as do many of the *dhows* in the Creek.

### Baniyas Square

This busy commercial square and traffic junction is the heart of Deira's business district and is home to airlines, hotels, restaurants, *shwarma* stands and businesses. By night, it glows with Tokyo-esque neon lights and signs. The Dubai Department of Tourism and Commerce Marketing has a useful Visitors Information Bureau here. The square is named after the influential Bani Yas tribe of Abu Dhabi, from which the ruling Maktoum family of Dubai is branched. ◈ *Map L2*

### Dhow Wharfs

A walk along the wharfside besides Baniyas Road allows you to get up close to the painted wooden *dhows*, the traditional Arabian sailing vessels, moored here. These ships still trade around the Gulf. Their cargo these days is tyres, refrigerators, air conditioners, electronics – just about any modern item! Moored five or six abreast, these *dhows* have sailed to trade with Dubai from places such as Iran, Pakistan and Sudan since the 1830s. ◈ *Map K3 • Baniyas Rd*

### Dubai Creek Golf & Yacht Club

This soaring white building, inspired, like the Burj Al Arab, by the sails of a *dhow*, and sitting amidst rolling greens, is a city landmark, visible from both

Maktoum and Garhoud bridges. Opened in January 1993, the world-class golf course here is the centre-piece of a sprawling leisure complex that also incorporates a 115-berth marina. The separate yacht club incorporates the Aquarium, an excellent seafood restaurant, as well as one of Dubai's most popular alfresco eateries, the Boardwalk *(see p64)*, which sits on stilts and offers a spectacular view of the Creek, especially at night when the illuminated *dhows* pass by. ◈ *Map K6 • Garhoud • 04 295 6000*

**National Bank of Dubai**
Another architectural achievement is the National Bank of Dubai – one of the city's first iconic buildings. Built in the mid-1990s by Carlos Ott, architect of the Opéra de la Bastille in Paris, it is inspired by the *dhow*. Its curved curtain glass wall symbolizes the billowing sail. The base of the building is clad in green glass representing water and its roof is aluminium, the hull of the boat. It is most striking at sunset, when the mirror reflects its gold and silver lights. ◈ *Map K3 • Baniyas Rd*

**National Bank of Dubai's stunning façade**

## A Souk Stroll

### Afternoon

🕐 Aim to start this walk around 4:30pm, when the souq shops re-open after prayers and temperatures are cooler. Start with an *abra* crossing from the **Bur Dubai Abra Station**. You can disembark at **Deira Old Souq Abra Station** *(see pp10–11)*. Take the underpass beneath **Baniyas Road** to emerge at the **spice souq** entrance. Enjoy a browse among the fragrant alleyways here. Leave the spice souq at **Al-Abra St**, turn right along **Al-Ras St** which leads into **Sikkat Al-Khail St**. Ahead you will see the latticed entrance to the **Gold Souq** with its colonnaded interior *(see p59)*. There are more than 300 jewellery shops to explore (most take credit cards). Wander into the alleyways off the main thoroughfare and enjoy a cup of tea at one of the small cafés. Exit at the gold souq and continue along Sikkat Al-Khail St to the tiny **Perfume Souq**. The shop windows here are a treasure trove of bottles filled with heady Arabian scents, incense and oud.

### Evening

🏵 Enjoy an evening snack by continuing along Sikkat Al-Khail St to **Ashwaq Cafeteria** *(see p64)*, a down-to-earth café with outdoor tables, serving shwarmas. Next, return to the **Creek** to admire the **Dhow Wharfage** *(see p84)*. For a relaxed end-of-day, drop in at **Radisson SAS Hotel's Up on the Tenth** *(see p65)* and chill with a cocktail and sensational sunset Creek views.

Left **Al Ghurair City's entrance** Centre **Textiles at Pride of Kashmir** Right **Paris Gallery's displays**

# Malls & Shops

### 1 Deira City Centre
This lively mall has 340 shops, an 11-screen cinema, a kid's entertainment area and good restaurants. ◈ *Map L5 • Garhoud, Deira • 04 295 1010 • Open 10am–10pm Sun-Wed, 10am–midnight Thu–Sat • www.deiracitycentre.com*

### 2 Al Ghurair City
A mall with an Arabic feel, this is Dubai's oldest. You can shop for international as well as local brands here. ◈ *Map L3 • Al Rigga Rd, Deira • 04 222 5222 • Open 10am–10pm Sun–Thu, 5pm–10pm Fri • www.alghuraircity.com*

### 3 Paris Gallery
Bvlgari, Dior, Chanel – you name the perfume of your choice and you'll find it at this upmarket store which also stocks a vast range of cosmetics, sunglasses and jewellery. ◈ *Map L5 • Floor 2, Stand E39, Deira City Centre • 04 295 5550 • www.uae-parisgallery.com*

### 4 Damas, City Centre
Visit for a choice of branded jewellery and watches, including Faberge, Chaumet and Vacheron Constantin. Mikimoto pearls are a speciality. ◈ *Map L5 • Floor 1, Stand C28, Deira City Centre • 04 295 3848 • www.damasjewel.com*

### 5 Al Jaber Gallery
An Aladdin's cave of treasures, this is a great store for souvenir-hunting. ◈ *Map L5 • Floor 1, Stand B3, Deira City Centre • 04 295 4114*

### 6 Pride of Kashmir
Presented as a mock souq, this store is packed with a wide selection of antique and modern rugs from Iran, Kashmir and Turkey, plus soft furnishings. Pick up a pashmina here, too. ◈ *Map L5 • Floor 1, Stand B9, Deira City Centre • 04 295 0655*

### 7 Ajmal
Specializing in Arabic perfumes, which are stronger and spicier than Western fragrances, this store will also mix you a signature scent that you can design with the in-house perfumier. ◈ *Map L5 • Floor 1, Stand B24, Deira City Centre • 04 295 3580*

### 8 Magrudy's
If you're looking for a good read, this well-stocked bookstore is your best bet. ◈ *Map L5 • Floor 2, Stand E20, Deira City Centre • 04 295 7744 • www.magrudy.com*

### 9 Plug-Ins
With tax-free shopping in Dubai, electronic goods can be a good buy. This electronic giant stocks everything, from printers and lap-tops to cameras and TVs. ◈ *Map L5 • Floor 2, Stand F1, Deira City Centre • 04 295 0404 • www.plug-ins.cc*

### 10 Reef Mall
Especially good for home furnishings and children's wear, you'll find both the high street brands as well as the economical ones here. ◈ *Map M3 • Salahuddin St • 04 224 2240 • www.reefmall.com*

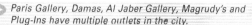

*Paris Gallery, Damas, Al Jaber Gallery, Magrudy's and Plug-Ins have multiple outlets in the city.*

**Price Categories**

For a three-course meal for one with half a bottle of wine (or equivalent meal), taxes and extra charges.

| | |
|---|---|
| **D** | Under AED 25 |
| **DD** | AED 25–100 |
| **DDD** | AED 100–150 |
| **DDDD** | AED 150–250 |
| **DDDDD** | Over AED 250 |

Left **Café Chic's French cuisine** Right **The stylish interior at China Club**

# Restaurants

### Verre
Dubai's most consistent fine dining experience. Gordon Ramsay's team is the best in town. Try the *degustation* menu. ⬥ *Map K3 • Hilton Dubai Creek, Baniyas St • 04 227 1111 • Open 7pm–11pm Sun–Fri • DDDDD*

### Café Chic
French dining, mellow jazz and a menu by a Michelin-starred chef – don't miss the soufflé. ⬥ *Map L6 • Le Meridien Dubai, Garhoud • 04 282 4040 • Open 12:30pm–2:45pm & 8pm–11:45pm • DDDD*

### China Club
This elegant restaurant has crisp table linen, striking oriental decor and an extensive menu of dim sum and Chinese classics. ⬥ *Map K2 • Radisson Deira Creek • 04 222 7171 • Open 12:30pm–3pm & 7:30pm–11pm • DDD*

### Glasshouse Mediterranean Brasserie
Gordon Ramsay's chic, glass-enclosed casual restaurant serves comfort food classics. Excellent for lunch or an informal dinner. ⬥ *Map K3 • Hilton Dubai Creek • 04 227 1111 • Open 7am–midnight • DDD*

### Traiteur
Relish the classic European cuisine as you admire the striking decor. ⬥ *Map K5 • Park Hyatt Hotel, Dubai Creek Club • 04 602 1234 • Open noon–3:30pm & 7pm–midnight • DDDDD*

### The Cellar
Have a pleasant alfresco lunch overlooking the lake of The Aviation Club or a romantic dinner inside the Gothic interior. ⬥ *Map L6 • The Aviation Club, Garhoud • 04 282 9333 • Open noon–2am • DDDD*

### Miyako
Stop by this tiny eatery for a sublime Japanese meal and impeccable service. ⬥ *Map L1 • Hyatt Regency Hotel, near Dubai Corniche • 04 317 2222 • Open 12:30pm–3pm & 7pm–midnight • DDDDD*

### M's Beef Bistro
Carnivores will rejoice at all the meaty dishes served here. Vegetarian options available. ⬥ *Map L6 • Le Meridien Hotel, near Airport • 04 282 4040 • Open 12:30pm–2:45pm & 8pm–11:45pm Sat–Thu, closed for lunch on Fri • DDDD*

### Ashiana
Experience colonial India at Ashiana. A chance to sample exquisite cooking within an empire-inspired decor of dark woodwork and golden lanterns. ⬥ *Map K3 • Sheraton Dubai Creek • 04 228 1111 • Open 12:30pm–3:30pm & 7:30pm–1:30am Sat–Thu, 7:30pm–1:30am Fri • DDDD*

### Blue Elephant
A must-visit for traditional Thai decor, delicious Thai food and a warm Thai welcome. ⬥ *Map L6 • Al Bustan Rotana Hotel, Al Garhoud Road • 282 0000 • Open noon–3pm & 7pm–11:30pm • DDD*

Left **Kiku's minimalist decor** Centre **A noodle dish at YUM!** Right **Fishy dishes at Creekside**

# Casual Eateries & Cafés

### 1 Thai Kitchen
The convenient tasting portions here allow you to sample many Thai delicacies from the four live cooking areas. ◎ *Map K5 • Park Hyatt Hotel, near Dubai Creek Golf Club • 04 602 1234 • Open 7pm–midnight • DDD*

### 2 YUM!
"Live Fast: Eat Fast" is this noodle kitchen's motto. Inspired by different Far Eastern cuisines, it makes for a fun pit stop! ◎ *Map L2 • Radisson Deira Creek • 04 222 7171 • Open noon–1am • DD*

### 3 Creekside
Savour the freshest of fish, expertly prepared Japanese style at this elegant restaurant with its teppanyaki station and sushi-sashimi bar and terrace tables with creek-side views. ◎ *Map K3 • Sheraton Dubai Creek • 04 228 1111 • Open 12:30pm–3pm & 6:30pm–11:30pm Sat–Thu, 6:30pm–11:30pm Fri • DDDD*

### 4 La Moda
Try some of the great Italian classics with a twist in a stylish setting. The wine list is expansive. ◎ *Map L2 • Radisson SAS Hotel • 04 222 7171 • Open 12:30pm–3pm & 7:30pm–2:30am • DDDD*

### 5 Casa Mia
It is "buon appetito" at this homely Italian restaurant, with a rustic decor and fresh breads, pastas and pizzas. ◎ *Map L6 • Le Meridien Dubai • 04 282 4040 • Open 12:30pm–3pm & 8pm–11:30pm • DDDDD*

### 6 Boardwalk
Built on a wooden veranda over the Creek, with stunning views, especially by night. The menu is varied with light Mediterranean fare and Eastern-inspired dishes. ◎ *Map K6 • Dubai Creek Golf & Yacht Club • 04 295 6000 • Open 8am–midnight • DDD*

### 7 Kiku
Ask to sit in a private tatami room for an intimate Japanese set meal of sushi, teppanyaki, sashimi and tempura. ◎ *Map L6 • Le Meridien Dubai • 04 282 4040 • Open 12:30pm–3pm & 7pm–11pm • DDDD*

### 8 More Café
This bustling all-day café serves up delicious home-style soups, salads and sandwiches, served mainly at long communal tables or on the outdoor terrace. ◎ *Map L6 • Next to Welcare hospital, behind Lifco super-market in Garhoud • 04 283 0224 • Open 7:30am–12:30am • No alcohol • DD*

### 9 Café Havana
Dig into a light lunch or relax on a couch with a cup of tea, warm scones, sandwiches and pastries. ◎ *Map L5 • City Centre, Deira • 04 295 5238 • Open 8am–midnight • DD*

### 10 Ashwaq Cafeteria
Settle yourself at an outdoor table for some great falafels, shwarmas and fresh juices. ◎ *Map K1 • Corner Al Soor St and Sikkat Al Khalil St, Deira • D*

*Recommend your favourite café on traveldk.com*

Left **The dining area at Up On the Tenth** Right **The Dubliners' eye-catching exterior**

# 🔟 Bars, Pubs & Clubs

### 1 The Terrace
Made for alfresco drinking and set on the marina front, The Terrace features the Raw Bar, offering a selection of caviar, oysters, prawns and salmon accompanied by an assortment of premium vodkas. 🚫 *Map K5* • Park Hyatt Hotel, Dubai Creek Golf Club • 04 317 2222 • *Open noon–1am*

### 2 Vista Lounge
This stylish bar in the new InterContinental hotel *(see p114)* has stunning views of the Creek and an interesting selection of cocktail creations. 🚫 *Map E3* • *InterContinental Dubai Festival City, Deira* • 04 701 1111

### 3 Up On the Tenth
The twinkling vistas, live jazz and sophisticated atmosphere will liven up your meal. 🚫 *Map L2* • Radisson SAS Hotel, Baniyas Rd, Deira • 04 205 7333 • *Open 6:30pm–3am*

### 4 Issimo
It's martini-heaven at this retro-futuristic cocktail bar. A great selection of spirits makes this an ideal after-dinner stop. 🚫 *Map L3* • Hilton Dubai Creek, Deira • 04 205 7333 • *Open 7pm–1am*

### 5 Irish Village
Throw back a pint or two, along with some fish and chips in Guinness batter, at this Irish-style pub with outdoor bench seating amidst greenery. 🚫 *Map L6* • Garhoud, Dubai • 04 282 4750 • *Open 11am–1am Fri-Tue & 11am–2am Wed-Thu*

### 6 QDs
Lounge at this Creekside wooden-decked terrace bar with a sundowner or chill with a hookah at the majlis area while the live band plays. 🚫 *Map K6* • Dubai Creek & Yacht Club • 04 295 6000 • *Open 5pm–2am*

### 7 The Dubliners
Another Irish pub that is always packed with expat residents. Inside, it's dark and cosy; outside there's a pleasant patio. A big choice of beers here. 🚫 *Map L6* • Le Meridien Hotel, near Airport • 04 282 4040 • *Open 11am–3am* • *Happy Hours 5pm–8pm*

### 8 KuBu
Abstract art covers the walls of this late-night night club serving a speciality choice of cocktails. The choice of music varies each night according to the DJ but house is big. 🚫 *Map L2* • Radisson SAS Hotel • 04 205 7333 • *Open 6pm–3am*

### 9 The Cellar
A restaurant and a bar with an extensive wine list, this venue has a pleasant outside space overlooking a tranquil lake *(see p63)*.

### 10 Oxygen
A long-established favourite with the locals. Expect R&B, hip hop and house, though the music varies each night. 🚫 *Map L6* • Al Bustan Rotana Hotel, Al Garhoud Road • 04 282 0000 • *Open 6pm–3am*

Left **Dubai Museum & Al Fahidi Fort** Right **Sheikh Juma Al-Maktoum House**

# Bur Dubai

THIS BUSTLING PART OF THE CITY IS *now packed with hotels, office block and residential developments, yet over a century ago it was an area of sand and barasti (palm frond houses) and windtower houses around the Creek. The best spot to get a real sense of old Bur Dubai is the historic Bastakiya quarter where the charming courtyard houses have been restored beside the Creek. This lovely atmospheric district is a quiet oasis amidst the city's hustle and bustle. Here too is the imposing Al Fahidi Fort, now Dubai Museum, the original defence outpost for Dubai. The Shindagha heritage area, right at the Creek mouth, is the spot where Dubai's role as an enterprising and cosmopolitan trading city really began. Bur Dubai's souqs, beginning with the textile- and curio-filled old Bur Dubai creekside souq are evidence of this. If you explore the streets further back, into the heart of the dizzyingly-colourful Textile Souq, you'll find a real community feel.*

**Bur Dubai Souq**

## 🔟 Sights

1. Dubai Museum & Al Fahidi Fort
2. Bastakiya
3. Heritage Village & Diving Village
4. Sheikh Saeed Al-Maktoum House
5. Sheikh Juma Al-Maktoum House
6. Sheikh Obaid bin Thani House
7. Bin Zayed Mosque
8. Bait Al Wakeel
9. Bur Dubai Souq
10. Ruler's Court/Diwan

### 1 Dubai Museum & Al Fahidi Fort

Once Dubai's main defence outpost, the imposing sand-coloured Al Fahidi Fort was built in 1788 and has also served as a gaol and the ruler's residence. Renovated in 1970, it is now the city museum and worth a visit for an informative overview of the emirate's history. It makes an entertaining visit for all ages: you can walk through a souq from the 1950s, visit an oasis with a *falaj* (irrigation channel), learn about the desert at night and visit a traditional *barasti* (palm frond) house *(see pp8–9)*.

### 2 Bastakiya

Now undergoing sympathetic restoration, this is one of the oldest and most atmospheric heritage areas in Dubai. Here you can wander the alleyways between original courtyard houses, many crowned by *barjeel* (windtowers) which were the earliest forms of air conditioning. Late afternoon is the best time to spend a couple of hours here, when the light throws the architecture into golden relief. The area has become a cultural hub for the city with many buildings converted to art galleries and courtyard cafés *(see pp12–13)*.

### 3 Heritage Village & Diving Village

A microcosm of Dubai's cultural and historic past, located near the mouth of the Creek in the old Shindagha conservation area, this traditional complex is a living museum staffed by potters and weavers practising crafts as they have for centuries. There's a tented Bedouin village, armoury displays, handicraft shops, camel rides and an exhibition of Emirati cooking techniques. The Diving Village focuses on Dubai's sea-faring and pearl diving history, with displays of traditional *dhows* and black and white photographs. ◈ *Map K1 • Al Shindagha • 04 393 7151 • Open 9am–9pm*

### 4 Sheikh Saeed Al-Maktoum House

Built in 1896 from coral stone covered in lime and sand plaster, this was the home of Dubai's former ruler until his death in 1958. The house was opened as a museum in 1986 and houses collections of photographs, coins, stamps and documents. It's worth visiting for the building itself, with its four windtowers and verandahs. Photographs from the 1950s–80s show seaplanes landing in the Creek and reveal the extraordinary pace of development. Copies of early oil prospecting agreements with international companies make fascinating reading on the Trucial Coast "oil rush". ◈ *Map J1 • Al Shindagha • 04 393 7139 • Open 8am–10pm Sat–Thu, 3pm–10pm Fri • Adm*

**A windtower in Bastakiya**

Around Dubai – Bur Dubai

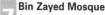

**Maktoum family's settlement on Dubai Creek**

The Maktoum family's reign as rulers of Dubai began in 1833, when Sheikh Maktoum bin Buti and around 800 tribesmen broke away from the Bani Yas tribe of Abu Dhabi. They settled in Shindagha, an ideal location for trade and for the development of Dubai's pearling and fishing industries.

 **Sheikh Juma Al-Maktoum House**

This building is a superb example of Arab structural design. Built in 1828, the rooms help you learn about the indigenous building materials used – mountain stone, mud, coral stone and gypsum – and the importance of the windtowers for internal cooling. ◎ *Map J1 • Al Shindagha • Open 8am–2:30pm Sun–Thu*

 **Sheikh Obaid bin Thani House**

This important property belonged to an influential member of the Qatari royal family who married into the Maktoum clan. A magnificent two-storey house with a courtyard, it was built in 1916. Offset entrances were designed to protect the privacy of the residents. The upper floor has larger openings to draw in the Creek breezes. The large lamp over the entrance harks back to the house's seafaring trading past. ◎ *Map K1 • Al Shindagha • Open 9am–2pm Sun–Thu*

**Bin Zayed Mosque**

An unusual square mosque without a traditional dome, the Bin Zayed Mosque was built in 1968. This spartan little place of worship is still used today. Close by is Al Mulla Mosque, made from mud and topped by a cylindrical minaret – restored according to the oral accounts of elderly Emiratis. ◎ *Map J1 • Al Shindagha*

**Bait Al Wakeel**

A fine example of early 20th-century coral stone architecture, the beautiful Bait Al Wakeel was once the offices of the British East India Shipping Company. This early office building, the first building in Dubai built specifically for administration, is worth a visit to check out the primitive facilities that Dubai's bureaucracy had to contend with. To the rear of the building is a casual eatery offering Creekside views. They offer decent Thai and Arabic

The Ruler's Court/Diwan at dusk

**Beautiful street lamps at the Textile Souq**

dishes on their menu, and it is well worth taking time out and stopping here for a juice or coffee to enjoy the bustling Creek vistas *(see p11)*.

**9 Bur Dubai Souq**

This souq begins at the water's edge by the Dubai Old Souq Abra Station and, since its renovation, is now housed under an imposing arcaded wooden roof. It's a mix of old and new – here you'll find moneychangers, textiles, bargain clothes, glittery Arabian slippers and curios. This souq merges with the Textile Souq, which is fun to explore – here you'll see tailors working on old-fashioned sewing machines *(see p21)*.

**10 Ruler's Court/Diwan**

A handsome cream building with imposing windtowers sits beside the Creek next to Bastakiya quarter and the Grand Mosque. The striking gold-topped wrought iron gates give a clue to its importance: this is the seat of power and is the Ruler's Court or *Diwan*, (Persian for couch). This is where Dubai's ruler Sheikh Mohammed's offices are located. ⊗ *Map K2 • Adjacent to Bastakiya, Creekside*

## A Day's Exploration of Old Dubai

### Morning

🕙 Start your tour at the **Heritage and Diving Village** at 10am, where you can learn about Emirati crafts and the history of Dubai's pearling industry. Break for fresh lemon and mint juice at any of the nearby waterside restaurants. Now head in the opposite direction to explore the rest of the **Shindagha heritage area**, including a visit to the museum within **Sheikh Saeed Al-Maktoum House** *(see pp10–11)*. Following the curve of the Creek you will arrive at the wooden-arcaded **Bur Dubai Souq**. Enjoy a browse of the textile and curio stalls here. Also, peep down the alleyways for views of restored windtowers and small fabric and tailor shops. At the end of the first covered section of the souq, head left to the Creek for a great view across to **Deira Spice Souq** *(see p20)*. Then wend your way through to **Ali Bin Abi Thalib Rd** – to your right is the unmistakable **Al Fahidi Fort and Dubai Museum** *(see pp8–9)*, where you can easily spend an interesting, informative hour.

### Afternoon

Head along **Al-Fahidi St** to the **Bastakiya** area where you can enjoy a leisurely courtyard lunch inside the restored building of the **Basta Art Café**. Afterwards, spend some time exploring Bastakiya's alleys and buildings; don't miss **Bastakiah Nights** and the **Majlis Gallery** *(see pp12–13)*.

Left **The atrium at Bur Juman** Right **A stained glass Egyptian panel at Wafi City**

# 🔟 Places to Shop

### Bur Dubai Souq
This souq starts at the creekside beneath a traditional wooden arcade. Wander through this old renovated souq with small shops and stalls selling a medley of goods from textiles to shoes to bargain clothing to curios *(see pp66–9)*.

### Bur Juman Mall
This chic shopping mall caters to those with money, with stores selling exclusive labels and glam accessories. ✆ *Map J3 • Trade Centre Rd • 04 352 0222 • Open 10am–10pm Sat–Thu, 4pm–10pm Fri*

### Al Orooba Oriental
If you are looking for an exotic gift, this is where you'll find top-quality Arabian souvenirs. They are sourced from as far afield as Iran, Pakistan, Kashmir and Kyrgistan. ✆ *Map J3 • 2nd floor, Bur Juman • 04 351 0919 • Open 12:30pm–3pm & 6:30pm–11:30pm Sat–Thu, 6:30pm–11:30pm Fri*

### Wafi City
This kitsch, Egyptian-themed, pyramid-shaped building is the place to head if you love fashion. ✆ *Map H5 • Oud Metha Rd • 04 324 4426 • Open 10am–10pm Sat–Thu, 4pm–10pm Fri*

### Amzaan
Specializing in funky foreign and Emirati labels, this uber-chic fashionista boutique is a real gem. ✆ *Map H5 • Wafi City • 04 324 6754 • Open 12:30pm–3pm & 8pm–11:30pm*

### Wafi Gourmet
Stocked to the ceiling with Arabian cheeses and sweets, barrels of the plumpest olives, dates and truffles, plus boxes of delectable Lebanese pastries and chocolates, it's no surprise that this is Dubai's favourite delicatessen. ✆ *Map H5 • Wafi City • 04 324 4555 • Open 8am–midnight*

### Five Green
This concept boutique, which combines eclectic clothing and music with an art gallery, is the city's answer to all things hip and edgy, with rails dominated by independant, young, urban designers. ✆ *Map J4 • Oud Metha, Garden Home Centre • 04 336 4100 • Open 12:30pm–3pm & 7pm–11pm*

### Praias
Choose from hundreds of the most gorgeous Brazilian bikinis and beach accessories here. ✆ *Map J3 • Bur Juman Mall • 04 351 1338 • Open 10am–10pm Sat–Thu, 4pm–10pm Fri*

### Karama "souq"
Hunt for cheap Arabian souvenirs, handicrafts and fake designer goods at this shopping complex. For local flavour, wander around the gritty neighbourhood afterwards *(see pp20–21)*.

### Satwa
This suburb is known for its fabrics, tailors and Indian sweet shops – where the local people shop *(see pp20–21)*.

**Price Categories**

For a three-course
meal for one with half
a bottle of wine (or
equivalent meal), taxes
and extra charges.

| | |
|---|---|
| **D** | Under AED 25 |
| **DD** | AED 25–100 |
| **DDD** | AED 100–150 |
| **DDDD** | AED 150–250 |
| **DDDDD** | Over AED 250 |

Left **An authentic Indian spread at Mumtaz Mahal**

# 🔟 Restaurants & Cafés

### 1 Fire & Ice

This place might resemble a Manhattan-style steakhouse with an identity crisis but there is no crisis of confidence in the kitchen. ✎ *Map H6 • Raffles Dubai • 04 324 8888 • Open 7pm–1am • DDDDD*

### 2 Peppercrab

Devour a tasty, peppery crab at this Singaporean superb seafood restaurant (aprons and pliers provided). ✎ *Map K5 • Park Hyatt Hotel, Dubai Creek Golf Club • 04 317 2222 • Open noon–1am • DDDDD*

### 3 Asha's

Bollywood singing sensation Asha Bhosle's glamorous restaurant has a loyal local following for its Indian classics, daring contemporary creations and equally adventurous cocktail list. ✎ *Map H5 • Pyramids Wafi City • 04 324 4100 • Open 12:30pm–3:30pm & 7:30pm–2am • DDDDD*

### 4 Manhattan Grill

Dig into high-quality juicy steaks at this American diner-styled restaurant. Set menu and vegetarian options are available too. The wine list here is generous. ✎ *Map J6 • Grand Hyatt • 04 317 1234 • Open 7pm–1am • DDDDD*

### 5 Medzo

This stylish Italian-influenced Mediterranean restaurant offers up an imaginative menu in a chic setting. ✎ *Map H5 • Wafi City • 04 324 4100 • Open 12:30pm–3pm & 7:30pm–11:30pm • DDDD*

### 6 Mumtaz Mahal

Dine here for an intimate Indian meal with traditional live music and authentic cuisine. The *kulfi* desserts are delicious. ✎ *Map K2 • Arabian Courtyard • 04 351 9111 • Open 12:30pm–3pm & 7pm–3am Sat–Thu, 7pm–3am Fri • DDDDD*

### 7 Thai Chi

Experience Thailand here – authentic cuisine served amidst a bamboo decor. ✎ *Map H5 • Pyramids Wafi City • 04 324 4100 • Open 12:30pm–3pm & 7:30pm–midnight • Happy Hours: 5pm–8pm • DDDD*

### 8 Bastakiah Nights

Escape into the mystical world of the fabled "A Thousand and One Nights" at this atmospheric Arabic restaurant, where the flames of torches flicker in its courtyard setting. ✎ *Map K2 • Bastakiya • 04 353 7772 • Open 12:30pm–11.30pm • No alcohol • DDD*

### 9 Lemongrass

An innovative and affordable Thai restaurant where you can savour some fresh, authentic dishes. ✎ *Map H4 • Near Lamcy Plaza • 04 334 2325 • Open noon–11:30pm • No alcohol • DDDD*

### 10 Basta Art Café

You'll be delighted to have a light lunch or juice at this bougainvillea-clad historic courtyard. A memorable lunch stop. ✎ *Map K2 • Bastakiya • 04 353 5071 • Open 10am–10pm • No alcohol • DD*

Families enjoying the weekend at Za'abeel Park

# Sheikh Zayed Road

THE KEY ARTERY OF DUBAI, SHEIKH ZAYED RD *is the outset of the highway direct to Abu Dhabi. It's becoming known as "The Strip" because, just as in Las Vegas, this symbol of Dubai's meteoric development is flanked with the most innovative and contemporary of global architecture. Gleaming skyscrapers tower above the lines of traffic beneath. Symbolically too, the road is the path to the city's future visionary expansion programme. Coming up at Interchange One are the Burj Dubai, the world's tallest building and Business Bay, Dubai's very own Manhattan-to-be. Further out, industrial Al Quoz has become a hub for art galleries.*

Burj Dubai and Business Bay

## TOP 10 Sights

1. Za'abeel Park
2. Dubai World Trade Centre
3. Dubai International Financial Centre (The Gate)
4. Burj Dubai
5. Ras Al Khor Wildlife Sanctuary
6. Business Bay
7. Al Quoz Art Galleries
8. Nad Al Sheba Race Club
9. Art Space
10. Emirates Towers & Boulevard

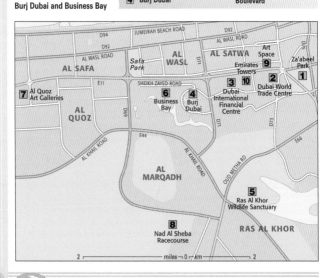

### 1 Za'abeel Park

Dubai's newest park is a delightful sea of green amidst the city's urban centre and offers spectacular views of the skyscraper-filled skyline of Sheikh Zayed Rd. This beautiful oasis boasts lakes, ponds, a jogging track, cricket pitch, football field, BMX track, play areas, shops and cafés. It is also the Middle East's first "technology park" and has three zones linked by pedestrian bridges: alternative energy, communications and technology, and a space maze based on the planetary system (see pp48–9). ⓢ Map F5–F6 • Sheikh Zayed Rd • 04 398 6888 • Open 8am–11pm Fri–Tue, 8am–11:30pm Wed–Thu

### 2 Dubai World Trade Centre

Hard to believe today when you see it dwarfed by the skyscrapers of Sheikh Zayed Rd, but back in 1979 the DWTC was the tallest building in the city, opened with great pomp by Sheikh Rashid and Queen Elizabeth II of England. It has played an important role in the city's development, a fact reflected by the continued use of its image on the AED 100 note. Today, it also comprises eight huge exhibition halls. The Dubai International Convention Centre next door can accommodate more than 6,500. ⓢ Map E5 • Sheikh Zayed Rd • 04 332 1000 • www.dwtc.com

### 3 Dubai International Financial Centre (The Gate)

Behind Emirates Towers is The Gate, the striking 15-storey architectural

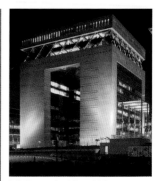
**Dubai International Financial Centre**

signature of the Dubai International Financial Centre (DIFC). The world's newest global financial hub was declared open for business in 2004. The Gate is shaped like a bridge – DIFC is designed to bridge the gap between the financial centres of London and New York in the West and Hong Kong and Tokyo in the East. ⓢ Map D6 • Sheikh Zayed Rd • 04 362 2222

### 4 Burj Dubai

"History rising" is how this futuristic glass tower pointing into the sky is being promoted. Now under construction, it is set to be the world's tallest building, overtaking the current title holder, Toronto's CN Tower. Its exact height is still under wraps but it will be over 700 m (2,300 ft) tall, with more than 160 floors. Scheduled for completion in 2009, its soaring design has challenged its architects, who admitted that "wind management" was their most critical engineering challenge. ⓢ Map C6 • Sheikh Zayed Rd • 04 367 5568

**World Trade Centre**

**Pink flamingos at Ras Al Khor**

### 5 Ras Al Khor Wildlife Sanctuary

Pink flamingos, waders and other birds can be viewed on a marshy reserve at the inner end of Dubai Creek. Managed by the World Wide Fund for Nature and the Emirates Wildlife Sanctuary, this urban reserve has three hides – Flamingo, Mangrove and Lagoon – designed as windtowers, all fitted out with telescopes, binoculars and picture panels. *Map E2 • Ras Al Khor • 04 206 4240 • Open 9am–4pm Sat–Thu • Free to the hides; groups of more than 10 require permits*

### 6 Business Bay

Business Bay, tipped to make Dubai a leading business capital of the stature of Manhattan, is a multi-billion dollar commercial development now underway with scores of ultramodern skyscrapers. It is set to attract huge foreign investment with hundreds of international companies setting up here in Dubai. Dubbed "a city within a city", its creation is so ambitious that a man-made waterway is currently under construction to connect with Ras Al Khor Wildlife Sanctuary. *Map B6 • Sheikh Zayed Rd • 04 391 1114*

### 7 Al Quoz Art Galleries

Al Quoz industrial district boasts the city's most cutting edge contemporary art galleries, including The Third Line, which exhibits provocative art and serious Middle East talent, and B21 Progressive Art Gallery, which is quickly developing a reputation for showing important work *(see p34)*.

### 8 Nad Al Sheba Race Club Tour

The early morning tour of these busy world-class stables includes a chance to see thoroughbred training in action. It starts with a full breakfast at the clubhouse, followed by a behind-the-scenes tour of the jockey centre, the weighing room and the farriers' facilities, the Millennium Grandstand and the Godolphin Gallery, where the Dubai World Cup stands proudly on display. *Map D3 • Nad Al Sheba • 04 336 3666 • Open 7am Sat, Mon, Wed • Adm • www.nadalshebaclub.com*

---

### Godolphin

Probably the most famous racing stable on the planet, Godolphin was established by the equestrian-enthusiast Maktoum Royal Family of Dubai in 1994 and has won Group One races in 11 countries. It bred the great Dubai Millennium, who won the Dubai World Cup 2000 by more than six lengths and sired 59 offspring. *www.godolphin.com*

### 9 Art Space

Dedicated to the promotion of mainly Emirati and Middle Eastern contemporary artists, this white-walled gallery with wooden floors caters to the taste and trends of the sophisticated Dubai art market. Contemporary art lovers will enjoy its high quality exhibitions. ⊕ *Map E5 • Fairmont Hotel, Sheikh Zayed Rd • 04 332 5523 • Open 10am–8:30pm Mon–Sun*

### 10 Emirates Towers & Boulevard

Two triangular twin towers, clad in aluminium and silver glass, soar into the Sheikh Zayed Road's skyline: the Jumeirah Emirates Towers. The taller is an office block, where Dubai Crown Prince Sheikh Mohammed bin Rashid Al Maktoum has his office, and the other a 400-bedroom luxury hotel joined by a central podium containing a shopping boulevard *(see p36)* and a 1,800 vehicle car park. The hotel has a great choice of restaurants and bars. ⊕ *Map D6 • Sheikh Zayed Rd, Dubai • 04 330 0000*

**Jumeirah Emirates Towers**

## A Shopping, Gallery & Spa Day

### Morning

Start your day with some shopping at the swanky **Emirates Towers** shopping boulevard, renowned for its designer stores. Now for some his and her pampering. He should head for **1847**, a classy gents salon, and ask for the 1847 shave – a 35-min old-fashioned treat that includes an oil massage, double shave and mask (Tel 330 1847, open 10am–10pm, AED 90, other treatments include facials and pedicures).

She should make a beeline for **N.Bar** where she can enjoy the combined manicure & pedicure treatment (Tel 330 1001, open 9am–9pm, AED 110). Leave the hotel and drive or take a taxi down the **Sheikh Zayed Rd** to the **Al Quoz** district after interchange no 3 (just before Mercedes-Benz showroom) where you'll find **The Third Line**, Dubai's most important art gallery exhibiting and selling works of art from the region and wider afield. Return to the Sheikh Zayed Rd and continue to the huge **Mall of the Emirates** *(see pp78–81)*. Plenty of choices for lunch here but the **Emporio Armani Caffè** is the most stylish spot *(see p84)*.

### Afternoon

Spend the afternoon browsing your favourite shops among more than 400 outlets here at Dubai's biggest retail centre. To rest your feet, catch a movie at the multi-screen cinema. If you are up for a bit of action, cool off with some skiing at **Ski Dubai** *(see pp78–81)*.

Left **Benjarong restaurant** Centre **Olive House** Right **Spectrum on One**

# 🔟 Restaurants & Cafés

### 1 Hoi An
Vietnamese fare served in elegant surroundings with superb cuisine and service. ◈ *Map C5 • Shangri-la Hotel • 04 343 8888 • www.shangri-la.com • DDDDD*

### 2 Marrakesh
Live Moroccan folk music accompanies dinner at this atmospheric restaurant. The mezzes and mains are both outstanding here. ◈ *Map C5 • Shangri-La Hotel • 04 343 8888 • www. shangri-la.com • DDDDD*

### 3 Vu's
This elegant fine dining restaurant on the 51st floor has food and vistas that are eye-catchingly engaging. ◈ *Map D6 • Emirates Towers • 04 319 8088 • www. jumeirah.com • DDDDD*

### 4 Benjarong
A Royal Thai restaurant, this offers impeccable Thai cuisine served in a regal atmos-phere. ◈ *Map C6 • Dusit Dubai • 04 343 3333 • www.dusit.com • DDDD*

### 5 Exchange Grill
This is the best steak restaurant in town – the culinary finesse combines the classic and the innovative. ◈ *Map E5 • Fairmont Hotel • 04 311 5999 • www. fairmont.com • DDDDD*

### 6 Spectrum on One
"Taste a nation" is the motto at this spacious multi-faceted restaurant offering a culturally diverse menu and global cuisine from numerous open kitchens. ◈ *Map E5 • Fairmont Hotel • 04 332 5555 • www.fairmont.com • DDDD*

### 7 Trader Vic's
This Polynesian restaurant is a local favourite – don't miss the exotic cocktails! ◈ *Map E5 • Crowne Plaza Hotel • 04 331 1111 • www.dubai.crowneplaza.com • DDDDD*

### 8 Noodle House
Visit for a quick, affordable and tasy bowl of spicy noodles. ◈ *Map D6 • Emirates Towers Shopping Boulevard • 04 319 8088 • www. jumeirah.com • DDD*

### 9 Tokyo@thetowers
Ultra-modern Japanese – eat on the tatami or at the sushi or teppanyaki bar. ◈ *Map D6 • Emirates Towers Shopping Boulevard • 04 319 8793 • www.jumeirah.com • DDDDD*

### 10 Olive House
Low priced fresh Lebanese-Mediterranean food make this Beirut-style café ideal for a quick meal. ◈ *Map C5 • Number One Tower, Sheikh Zayed Rd, Dubai • 04 343 3110 • DD; No alcohol*

**Price Categories**

For a three-course meal for one with half a bottle of wine (or equivalent meal), taxes and extra charges.

D Under AED 25
DD AED 25–100
DDD AED 100–150
DDDD AED 150–250
DDDDD Over AED 250

Left **The Agency bar** Right **The stylish Cin Cin's**

# 🔟 Bars & Clubs

### 1 The Agency
Choose from 50 different wines, served in a Manhattan-style ambience. ✪ *Map D6 • Emirates Towers Hotel • 04 319 8088 • www.jumeirahemiratestowers.com*

### 2 Vu's Bar
This sophisticated cocktail bar has unbeatable views and a selection of international cocktails. ✪ *Map D6 • Emirates Towers Hotel • 04 330 0000 • www.jumeirahemiratestowers.com*

### 3 Cin Cin's
This chic champagne bar has a sublime snack menu, featuring freshly-shucked oysters and Wagyu beefburgers. ✪ *Map E5 • Fairmont Hotel • 04 311 8316 • www.fairmont.com*

### 4 Lotus One
Groovy house DJs, chairs that swing on chains from the ceiling and an illuminated bar make this a stylish venue. ✪ *Map E6 • World Trade Convention Centre • 04 329 3200 • www.lotus1.com*

### 5 Blue Bar
Low-key relaxed bar where you can chill to the tunes of the resident jazz band. ✪ *Map E5 • Novotel Hotel, behind World Trade Centre • 04 332 0000*

### 6 Mai Tai Lounge
This bar boasts one of the longest and most exotic cocktail lists in the city. ✪ *Map E5 • Crowne Plaza Dubai • 04 331 1111 • www.crowneplaza.com*

### 7 Long's Bar
This colonial-style bar, with its small dance floor, claims to have the longest bar in the UAE. ✪ *Map D5 • Towers Rotana Hotel • 04 312 2202 • www.rotana.com*

### 8 Harry Ghatto's
Pure entertainment can be enjoyed at this lively Japanese karaoke bar offering over 1,000 songs to sing and great cocktails and drinks. ✪ *Map D6 • Emirates Towers Hotel • 04 330 0000 • www.jumeirah.com*

### 9 The Loft
A bar-club hybrid, The Loft has two levels and high ceilings and guarantees great DJ-ed music. The layout means you can choose between two vibes: settle back or party down. ✪ *Map E6 • Sheikh Zayed Rd • 050 846 3424*

### 10 Zinc
Always packed, this popular and lively club has an ever-changing line up of live music and local DJs. ✪ *Map E5 • Crowne Plaza Hotel • 04 331 1111 • www.crowneplaza.com*

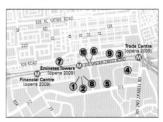

Left **Russian Beach** Right **Weekend market at Marina**

# Jumeirah & New Dubai

JUMEIRAH, A DISTRICT OCCUPYING THE PRIME BELT *of coastline stretching south-west from the port area, is the most glamorous and hedonistic of the city. It's no surprise that residential property here is pricey – it's the ultimate location for a villa in the sun and the quiet leafy streets are filled with bougainvillea-clad luxury villas, usually with a BMW or a monster four-wheel drive parked outside. Here too are the city's most extravagant resort hotels, including the Burj Al Arab, the wave-shaped Jumeirah Beach Hotel, the Arabian-styled One&Only Royal Mirage and the vast Madinat Jumeirah, plus a string of others stretching out along this all-important coastal strip of the Arabian Gulf. Out at sea is the famous Palm Jumeirah Island, whose villa-topped fronds have extended the coastline by 120km. The area is excellent for shopping and leisure and for enjoying beachlife in general, whether you choose to stretch out on your hotel beach or enjoy any of the public beaches.*

The impressive Mall of the Emirates

## Sights

1. Jumeirah Beach
2. Burj Al Arab
3. Madinat Jumeirah
4. Wild Wadi Water Park
5. Russian Beach
6. Safa Park
7. Jumeirah Beach Park
8. Ski Dubai
9. Mall of the Emirates
10. Marina Markets

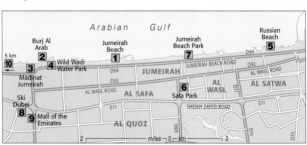

People soaking up the sun at a beach along Jumeirah

### Jumeirah Beach
Strictly speaking, Jumeirah Beach is the 9-km (6 miles) stretch of golden coastline running parallel to the Jumeirah Beach Rd, lined by some of the city's most desirable villa accommodation and hotels. There's a good choice of public beaches at Umm Suqueim, Kite Beach and Russian Beach, while the pleasant Jumeirah Beach Park is a delightful spot to while away a day in the sun. ◈ *Map A4 • Jumeirah*

### Burj Al Arab
Visible from almost anywhere in Jumeirah is the iconic luxury hotel, the Burj Al Arab, a symbol for the city itself and distinguished by its unusual shape mirroring the billowing sail of a *dhow*. Reservations are needed to visit the interior of this opulent hotel. For a great close-up view of the exterior, drop into the Jumeirah Beach Hotel *(see p44)* and take the super-fast glass elevator to the top floor *(see pp16–17)*.

### Madinat Jumeirah
This vast leisure and entertainment complex has become a major focus of the Jumeirah area – with its two hotels, Al Qasr and Mina A' Salam *(see pp18–19)* linked by a series of seawater-fed waterways navigated by silent battery-powered *abras*. There are more than 45 restaurants, bars and cafés, many offering waterside views, with the romantic seafood restaurant, Pierchic *(see p83)*, located on a pier that stretches into the Arabian Gulf. Here too you'll find the city's hippest dance club, Trilogy, plus the Madinat Jumeirah Souq, a delightful reconstruction of a traditional Arabian bazaar *(see pp18–19)*.

### Wild Wadi Water Park
This huge world-class water park offers a great day out to suit all ages and bravery levels with 31 water-fuelled rides and attractions. Thrill-seekers will not be disappointed by its most challenging ride, the Jumeirah Sceirah – it's the tallest and fastest freefall waterslide outside the US. Well staffed by lifeguards and with plenty of food outlets, it makes for a fun day out. ◈ *Map C1 • Jumeirah Beach Rd • 04 348 4444 • Sep–Oct & Mar–May 11am–7pm; Nov–Feb 11am–6pm; Jun–Aug 11am–9pm • Adm • www.wildwadi.com • There is a cashless payment system using an electronic waterproof wristband*

### Russian Beach

This is one of the city's best known and most crowded public beaches, especially at weekends and evenings. It's also known as Open Beach. The beach offers safe bathing and is divided by manmade breakwaters – useful on windy days – and is well-placed for you to be able to wander off for lunch or a drink at nearby Palm Strip Shopping Mall *(see p82)* or the malls on the other side of Beach Rd. ◉ *Map D4*

### Safa Park

You can't miss the giant Ferris wheel here, offering the best views of this huge land-scaped green park stretching from Al Wasl Rd to Sheikh Zayed Rd. It is hugely popular with local residents, many of whom make the most of its specially-sprung perimeter jogging track. It's great for kids to run free and there's lots of entertainment too with tennis courts, trampolining, mini train, a merry-go-round, obstacle course and lake where rowing boats can be hired. ◉ *Map A5*

### Jumeirah Beach Park

This lovely green park, full of mature trees, backs onto a beautiful stretch of white sand beach. It is a real gem and an ideal place to spend a day in the sun, although weekends are best avoided when it gets crowded. You can access the beach from the park along wooden walkways and there is plenty of shade on the sand under the many palm trees. It's great for children and is equipped with lifeguards, a shallow beach, showers, toilets, barbecues, picnic tables and small cafés. ◉ *Map A4*

### Ski Dubai

You can't miss Ski Dubai from the Sheikh Zayed Rd, jutting out like a giant space-age tube. Holding over 6,000 tonnes

The green Safa Park

**Ski Dubai**

of snow, it offers five slopes linked by chairlifts and tow lifts to cater to all ski levels, including the longest black indoor run in the world. There's also a snow park for little ones. Ski gear is provided in the ticket *(see p32)*.

**9 Mall of the Emirates**

This is Dubai's swankiest retail complex, with more than 400 shops, selling every product you can possibly dream of. There's also a huge branch of Carrefour supermarket, Harvey Nichols and Debenhams, plus myriad fashion labels. It has a multi-screen cinema and big kids' play area, Magic Planet, plus dozens of cafés and restaurants. ◎ *Map C2*
• *Interchange 4 • 04 409 9000 • www. malloftheemirates.com*

**10 Marina Markets**

Dubai Marina is a stunning marina-side development of luxury apartment towers and offices. Unsurprisingly, alfresco waterside life has really taken off alongside the main pedestrian area, Marina Walk, where there are dozens of outdoor cafés. Friday sees the setting up of Marina Markets around the stunning central fountain and dancing water features and the arrival of dozens of colourful stalls selling art and handicrafts. It's a great chance to combine shopping with some sunshine. ◎ *Map B2*

## A Day by the Sea

### Morning

Start your day with breakfast on the outdoor terrace of **Lime Tree Café** *(see p84)*. Enjoy the gentle morning sun as you sip on some coffee or a juice. Drive or hire a taxi to **Jumeirah Beach Park** where you can take a safe swim. Follow it up with a picnic snack on the manicured lawns. If you want to simply laze about, you can hire a sunbed under the palmtrees and spend the morning relaxing in the sunshine. Leave at lunchtime and head to **Madinat Jumeirah** *(see pp18–19)* where you have a huge choice of restaurants at which to enjoy a leisurely late lunch, many overlooking the waterways. Afterwards spend an hour or two shopping for souvenirs or browsing the lovely Arabian-style **Madinat Jumeirah Souq** here.

### Evening

Now head to one of Dubai's most atmospheric resort venues, the **One&Only Royal Mirage's Arabian Court**, to the **Rooftop Bar** *(see p85)*. From this alfresco spot, you can sip a cocktail over superb views of **Palm Jumeirah Island** *(see p32)* and watch the sun set over the Gulf. For dinner head to the hotel's **Beach Bar & Grill**, a delightful Arabian-themed seafood restaurant located on decking right on the beach where you can enjoy the sound of the waves. It's worth booking a table here beforehand. The Beach Bar & Grill: One&Only Royal Mirage; 399 9999; DDDDD.

Left **Ibn Battuta's exotic interiors** Centre **The Village emblem** Right **Souq Madinat Jumeirah**

# Shopping Centres

### 1 Souq Madinat Jumeirah
A reconstruction of a traditional Arabian marketplace within atmospheric Madinat Jumeirah, this magical bazaar offers jewellery, antiques, handicrafts and art, interspersed with bars and restaurants *(see pp18–19)*.

### 2 Mall of the Emirates
Prepare to shop until you drop and grab a map when you arrive: you'll need it! This is one of the biggest shopping centres in the region with over 400 outlets and top names including Harvey Nichols, Debenhams and Carrefour *(see p81)*.

### 3 Ibn Battuta Mall
Great fun to visit, this themed mall, based on the journeys of Arabian traveller Ibn Battuta, has six shopping zones, food courts and a 21-screen cinema. ◈ *Map A2 • Emirates Hills • 04 362 1900 • www.ibnbattutamall.com*

### 4 Mercato Mall
Resembling a vast Italian film set, Mercato is an Italian-themed mall with 90 shops, restaurants and cafés. Good for kids with a fun city play area and an Early Learning Centre. ◈ *Map C4 • Jumeirah Beach Rd • 04 344 4161 • www.mercatoshoppingmall.com*

### 5 The Village Mall
An intriguing mix of niche upmarket boutiques fill this pretty shopping centre with its archways, plants and fountains. A good place for finding an exclusive gift. ◈ *Map D4 • Jumeirah Beach Rd • 04 344 7714*

### 6 Burj Al Arab
Tiny but full of exclusive designer brands, this is the only place you can buy authentic Burj Al Arab souvenirs *(see pp16–17)*.

### 7 Palm Strip
This pleasant outdoor mall is tiny in comparison to other retail megaliths and offers some up-market boutiques plus Mango, Zara Home, Karen Millen, La Senza, a nail bar and Japengo, a lively alfresco café. ◈ *Map E4 • Jumeirah Beach Rd • 04 346 1462*

### 8 Town Centre
A community mall much frequented by expats, there's a fun Café Céramique where you can design your own pottery. ◈ *Map C4 • Jumeirah Beach Rd • 04 344 0111 • www.towncentrejumeirah.com*

### 9 Jumeirah Plaza
Known as the "pink mall" for its frontage, this is a small shopping centre with a kids' play area and Dome Café. ◈ *Map D4 • Jumeirah Beach Rd • 04 349 7111*

### 10 Jumeirah Centre
This small mall, popular with local residents, has a pleasant coffee shop with outdoor terrace. Sunny Days, a boutique upstairs, sells handicrafts and gifts. ◈ *Map D4 • Jumeirah Beach Rd • 04 349 9702*

**Price Categories**

For a three-course meal for one with half a bottle of wine (or equivalent meal), taxes and extra charges.

| | |
|---|---|
| **D** | Under AED 25 |
| **DD** | AED 25–100 |
| **DDD** | AED 100–150 |
| **DDDD** | AED 150–250 |
| **DDDDD** | Over AED 250 |

Left **A table setting at Maya** Right **Indian cuisine with a twist at Nina**

# 🔟 Restaurants

### 1 Tajine

Visit this candlelit restaurant with live music and waiters in traditional dress for a magical Moroccan experience. Its location, from a courtyard within Dubai's most atmospheric Arabian hotel resort, adds to its charm. ✆ *Map B1* • *One&Only Royal Mirage, Al Sufouh* • *04 399 9999* • *www.oneandonlyroyalmirage.com* • *DDDD*

### 2 Maya

Experience new-wave Mexican cuisine within spacious surroundings decorated with Mayan art and modern sculpture. ✆ *Map B1* • *Le Royal Meridien Beach Resort & Spa* • *04 399 5555* • *DDDDD*

### 3 Zheng He's

The Chinese cuisine here focuses on fresh seafood. The harbour view is stunning. ✆ *Map C1* • *Mina A' Salam, Madinat Jumeirah* • *04 366 8888* • *DDDDD*

### 4 Nina

Sample traditional Indian ingredients with a new twist at this sophisticated restaurant within the lush surroundings of this Arabian resort. ✆ *Map B1* • *One&Only Royal Mirage* • *04 399 9999* • *DDDDD*

### 5 Pierchic

Definitely book a terrace table at this seafood restaurant situated on a wooden pier overlooking the Arabian Gulf. ✆ *Map C1* • *Al Qasr, Madinat Jumeirah* • *04 366 8888* • *DDDDD*

### 6 Indego

Expect a contemporary take on traditional Indian cuisine at this chic restaurant overseen by Vineet Bhatia, the first Indian chef to be awarded a Michelin star. ✆ *Map B2* • *Grosvenor House Hotel, Al Sufouh* • *04 399 8888* • *DDDDD*

### 7 Ottomans

Dine on Turkish cuisine in Ottoman decor with views over Dubai Marina. Ask for a terrace table so you can enjoy the water views. ✆ *Map B2* • *Grosvenor House Hotel* • *04 399 8888* • *DDDDD*

### 8 Shoo Fee Ma Fee

Feast on superb Moroccan cuisine then sit back with a bubbling sheesha on the terrace of this labyrinthine Moroccan restaurant overlooking the Madinat Jumeirah waterways. ✆ *Map C2* • *Souq Madinat Jumeirah* • *04 366 8888* • *DDDD*

### 9 BiCe

Wonderful Italian comfort food served at this hugely popular restaurant with live piano and huge windows overlooking the pool. ✆ *Map B1* • *Hilton Dubai, Jumeirah* • *04 399 1111* • *DDDDD*

### 10 Tang

Dubai's first restaurant to offer cuisine based on molecular gastronomy, Tang's tapas-size dishes delight the senses. ✆ *Map B1* • *Le Meridien Mina Seyahi* • *04 399 3333* • *DDDDD*

*Recommend your favourite restaurant on traveldk.com*

Left **Fusion food at Fudo** Centre **The popular Lime Tree Cafe** Right **Visit Finz for seafood**

# Cafés & Casual Eats

### 1 Almaz by Momo
The creative signature of Mourad Mazouz, founder of Soho London celebrity haunt Momo, is strong in this Moroccan restaurant. ⊗ *Map C2 • Mall of the Emirates • 04 409 8877 • Open 10am–midnight Sun-Thu, 10am–1:30am, Fri-Sat • No alcohol • DDD*

### 2 Emporio Armani Caffé
This is a super-sleek restaurant with classic Italian cuisine prepared by Italian chef Stefano Rutigliano. ⊗ *Map C2 • Mall of the Emirates • 04 341 0591 • DDD; no alcohol*

### 3 Toscana
Drop in with the kids for some delicious Italian fare served up in a lovely mock Venetian waterway setting at this family-friendly restaurant. ⊗ *Map C2 • Madinat Jumeirah • 04 366 8888 • DDD*

### 4 Bella Donna
Known for its excellent thin pizzas, you'll also find a wide choice of classic pasta dishes at this contemporary styled Italian eatery. ⊗ *Map C4 • Mercato Mall • 04 344 7701 • DD; no alcohol*

### 5 Chandelier
This casual Lebanese restaurant next to Dubai Marina's dancing fountain is good for a light lunch or evening meal. It has a pleasant outdoor terrace, where you can also sample sheesha. ⊗ *Map B1 • Dubai Marina • 04 366 3606 • DDD; no alcohol*

### 6 Lime Tree Café
This homely café with a shady outdoor garden terrace serves healthy homemade lunches, soups, juices, teas and coffees. The café is popular with the expat crowd. ⊗ *Map D4 • Jumeirah Beach Rd • 04 348 9498 • DD; no alcohol*

### 7 Maria Bonita's Taco Shop
A visit to Maria Bonita is like being transported to Mexico. This relaxed good-value restaurant serves great tacos, tortillas and salsas. ⊗ *Map C2 • Umm Al Sheif St • 04 395 4454 • DD; no alcohol*

### 8 Dome
Ask for the soup and sandwich of the day at this informal café with a pleasant terrace. It serves good coffee and juices too. ⊗ *Map C2 • Souq Madinat Jumeirah • 04 366 8888 • DD*

### 9 Fudo
Feast on fusion food from Lebanon, Japan, Thailand and Italy, with wonderful fruit cocktails at this off-street patio restaurant with leafy trees. ⊗ *Map C4 • Jumeirah Beach Rd, next to Mercato Mall • 04 344 8896 • DD; no alcohol*

### 10 Finz
This casual shopping centre eatery offers excellent value Mediterranean cuisine, including lobster ravioli and seafood bisque. ⊗ *Map A2 • Ibn Battuta Mall • 04 368 5620 • DD; no alcohol*

**Price Categories**

For a three-course meal for one with half a bottle of wine (or equivalent meal), taxes and extra charges.

| | |
|---|---|
| **D** | Under AED 25 |
| **DD** | AED 25–100 |
| **DDD** | AED 100–150 |
| **DDDD** | AED 150–250 |
| **DDDDD** | Over AED 250 |

Left **The Rooftop bar** Right **A window seat at the Skyview Bar**

# 🎖10 Bars & Clubs

### 1 The Rooftop
For a relaxed evening drink under a star-filled sky, this Moroccan-styled bar with its superb views over the Arabian Gulf makes for a memorable experience. ⬧ *Map B1 • Arabian Court, One&Only Royal Mirage • 04 399 9999 • Open 5pm–1am*

### 2 Bahri Bar
An ideal spot for a sun-downer with its wraparound terrace and views of the light shows of the Burj Al Arab. ⬧ *Map C2 • Madinat Jumeirah • 04 366 8888 • Open 2pm–11:30pm*

### 3 Sho Cho's
This super-chic Japanese bar offers a gorgeous terrace overlooking the Gulf and interior walls filled with fish tanks. ⬧ *Map E4 • Dubai Marine Beach Resort & Spa • 04 346 1111 • Open 7pm–3am*

### 4 Trilogy
An enormous dance floor, cutting-edge music and world-class DJs make this Arabian-style club on three levels pure hedonism and somewhere you can dance until the smallest hours. ⬧ *Map C2 • Madinat Jumeirah • 04 366 6917 • Open 9pm–3am*

### 5 Buddha Bar
Expect a chilled-out Asian vibe at this eastern-inspired cocktail bar with its tucked away alcoves and colossal Buddha centrepiece. ⬧ *Map B2 • Grosvenor House • 04 399 8888 • Open 8pm–2am*

### 6 Skyview Bar
Choose a window seat for the maximum experience at this 27th-floor cocktail bar where you can enjoy tailormade cocktails. The extravagant Burj Al Arab decor alone makes this bar worth a visit (*see pp16–17*). ⬧ *Map C1 • Burj Al Arab • 04 301 7438 • Open 11am–2am*

### 7 Bar 44
Forty-four different types of champagne are on offer at this top-floor swanky bar with intimate sofas and a giant balcony. ⬧ *Map B2 • Grosvenor House • 04 317 6871 • Open 6pm–2am*

### 8 The Agency
This wine bar offers "wine flights" – a chance to choose from 50 different connoisseur-selected wines. ⬧ *Map D6 • Boulevard, Emirates Towers • 04 330 0000 • Open 12:30pm–1am Sat–Thu, 3pm–1am Fri*

### 9 360 degrees
Located in a glass building perched out at sea at the end of a breakwater, this is ideal for a sunset drink. ⬧ *Map C1 • Jumeirah Beach Hotel • 04 406 8744 • Open 5pm–2am Sat–Wed, 4pm–2am Thu–Fri*

### 10 Koubba
A rooftop bar of elevated Arabian style offering champagne cocktails. Try the fabulous "espresso martini" for a real wake-up. ⬧ *Map C2 • Al Qasr, Madinat Jumeirah • 04 366 6743 • Open noon–2am*

*Recommend your favourite bar on traveldk.com*

Left **The skyline** Right **The murals at Lulu Island**

# Around Abu Dhabi

A STUNNING CITY OF SHINY SKYSCRAPERS LINING *a splendid Corniche*, oil-rich Abu Dhabi is the capital of Abu Dhabi emirate as well as of the UAE. Home to the excellent arts centre, the Abu Dhabi Cultural Foundation, it is also the country's cultural and intellectual capital. It is often compared to New York, with its more glamorous sister Dubai likened to LA. An island-city with plenty of narrow white sand beaches and crystal clear turquoise waters lapping at its shores, Abu Dhabi is popular with beachcombers and lovers of the outdoors. Local residents ritually power-walk along the city's waterfront. The median strips of its wide streets are planted with towering date palms, while its green parks are packed with playground equipment for kids.

A picnic at a public beach

## 🔟 Sights

1. Emirates Palace
2. Abu Dhabi Heritage Village
3. Abu Dhabi Corniche
4. Al Markaziyah Gardens
5. Al Bateen dhow-building yards
6. Women's Handicraft Centre
7. Public Beach
8. Lulu Island
9. Al Maqtaa Fort & Palace
10. Saadiyat Island

Previous pages **Sheikh Zayed Road, the key artery of Dubai**

**The magnificent Emirates Palace**

### Emirates Palace

Abu Dhabi's magnificent pink palace hotel dominates the western end of the splendid Corniche. The majestic multi-domed exterior is surpassed in extravagance by the dazzling interior, glittering with gold and sparkling with Swarovski crystals. Completed in 2005, it was constructed to provide opulent accommodation fitting for the capital's visiting dignitaries – from Saudi princes to world leaders to Hollywood stars *(see pp22–3)*.

### Abu Dhabi Heritage Village

The delightful Heritage Village provides a fascinating insight into what everyday life was like in Abu Dhabi before oil was discovered. A recreation of a traditional mosque, *barasti* house, Bedouin camp and souq are all worth a look, but the star sight is an intriguing museum set in a fort with fabulous exhibits featuring costumes, jewellery, everyday utensils, pearling tools and weapons. There's an arcade of artisan's workshops where you can watch basket weaving, glass blowing, weaving and brass-beating. ◈ *Map N5 • The Breakwater, next to the flagpole • 02 681 4455 • Open 8am–1pm & 5–9pm Sat–Thu, 5pm–9pm Fri*

### Abu Dhabi Corniche

The Corniche curves from one end of the city to the other. Wide enough to accommodate power-walkers, joggers, in-line skaters and cyclists, its paved path is lined with ice-cream dispensers and shady pavilions to escape the heat. ◈ *Map P5 • Corniche Rd • Open 24 hours*

### Al Markaziyah Gardens

In a city of wide, green parks, of which Capitol Gardens, Khalidiya Children's Gardens, Al Mushrif Childrens Gardens and Al Khubeirah Gardens stand out, the new Al Markaziyah Gardens is the city's most popular. Head here any time of the day during the cooler winter period, or in the evening during the steamy summer months, and the garden is packed. The parks are open to the public all day. ◈ *Map P4 • Between 1st St, Al Nasr St, Tariq Bin Zayed St & 26th St • Open 24 hours*

**The Corniche**

### Al Bateen Dhow-Building Yards

Boat lovers and admirers of traditional crafts should visit the fascinating *dhow*-building yards situated on an island connected to the land by a short causeway in Khor Al Bateen (Al Bateen Creek). The ramshackle huts and cluttered yards comprise the actual workplace of these boat builders, who lovingly handcraft these boats using traditional techniques. While they don't mind visitors watching and welcome the interest in their work, take them some cold drinks as a sign of appreciation. An early morning or late afternoon visit is best as they take a siesta at lunch. ⚓ *Map Q6 • Off Bainunah St, near Marina Sports Club*

### Women's Handicraft Centre

Watch veiled Bedouin women chatting to each other as they demonstrate basket-weaving, embroidery, textile making and henna art in a series of workshops at the rear of the Women's Union. You can also buy their work – which they would greatly appreciate. Browse through the displays of costumes, textiles and jewellery in the Exhibition Hall on your way out. Take your shoes off before entering the workshops and remember not to photograph the women without asking first. ⚓ *Women's Union, Al Karamah St • 02 447 6645 • Open 8:30am–1pm Sat–Wed*

### Public Beach

Join the locals for some sunbathing on the soft white sand or a swim in the crystal clear sea at the public beach at Ras Al Akhdar. Head here early morning for a dip in the warm water, when you might share the sand with horseriders exercising their mounts. The weekends see the city's workers here for games of cricket. It is advisable to dress modestly until you're on the beach itself. ⚓ *Map N6 • Ras Al Akhdar, past the Diwan, Corniche Rd West*

### Lulu Island

Visible from anywhere along Abu Dhabi's Corniche, Lulu Island is distinguished by its high red sand dunes and groves of date palms – and its enormous billboard-size portraits of the late UAE President Sheikh Zayed and the late Vice-President and Ruler of Dubai Sheikh Maktoum. While creation of the man-made island began in 1988, it's always been underutilized. That's soon set to

**Weaving at the Women's Handicraft Centre**

**Al Maqtaa Fort & Palace**

### Corniche & City Walk

**Morning**

🕐 Get a taxi in the early morning to the big flag pole at the tip of the **Breakwater** for views of the city skyline. Walk to the **Abu Dhabi Heritage Village** close by soon after opening, and spend time admiring the recreations of old souqs, Bedouin camps and barasti living quarters.

☕ Stop by a coffee shop on the white sand beach overlooking the city for a refreshment. You'll need to pick up the pace for a brisk walk around the Breakwater and along the causeway to the **Emirates Palace**. Take time to admire the jaw-dropping interior and refuel at the elegant coffee shop. Then continue along the **Corniche**, stopping to catch stunning views of **Lulu Island**.

**Afternoon**

When you get to Sheikh Rashid bin Saeed Al Maktoum St (2nd St) you'll see the signs to **Central Market** – head down here to look at the giant white iconic statues of Abu Dhabi's beloved symbols – a coffee pot, cannon, incense burner and perfume sprinkler. From here, cross the busy intersection with Al Nasr and Hamdan Sts to the **Cultural Foundation** for lunch at Delma Café *(see p25)*. After lunch, check out **Heritage Corner**. Grab a programme to see if there's a cultural performance in the evening that's worth returning for. Head back to the hotel for a well-earned siesta and then return to the Corniche to watch the beautiful sunset.

change with the construction of a wildlife reserve, museum, gardens and eateries. ◈ *Map N4*

**Al Maqtaa Fort & Palace**
This splendid 200-year old sand-coloured fort has intricately carved wooden doors and shuttered windows. It has one white watchtower on a tiny island in the sea and another on the other side of the bridge. A small museum is due to open inside soon. ◈ *Abu Dhabi-Dubai Rd; on the right before the bridge if driving from Dubai • Interior not open at time of research*

**Saadiyat Island**
Once a sleepy retreat for locals who liked to boat over to the island for a barbecue, Saadiyat Island (Island of Happiness) made international news when its redevelopment plans were unveiled. Set to be transformed into a world class cultural, entertainment and leisure precinct, the island will be home to a new Guggenheim Museum designed by Frank Gehry, a branch of the Louvre by Jean Nouvel, a performing arts centre by Zaha Hadid and a maritime museum by Tadao Ando. ◈ *www.saadiyat.ae*

Left **The "AD Mall"** Centre **Khalifa Centre's exotic ware** Right **Haggling at Madinat Zayed**

# 🔟 Places to Shop

### 1 Abu Dhabi Mall
Known popularly as "AD Mall", it has all the usual suspects when it comes to shops. ⊗ Map Q1 • Tourist Club area • 02 645 4858 • www.abudhabimall.com

### 2 Marina Mall
This enormous mall is packed with stores, cinemas, cafés and a snow dome. ⊗ Map N5 • The Breakwater • 02 681 8300 • www.marinamall.ae

### 3 Madinat Zayed Shopping Centre & New Gold "Souq"
Haggle for bargains at discount shops here as well as at the glitzy Gold Centre next door. ⊗ Map P2 • East Rd, near Main Post Office • 02 631 8555

### 4 Iranian Souq
Amidst the plastics and plants sold here, you'll find good Iranian painted crafts. ⊗ Map N1 • Mina (port)

### 5 Carpet Souq
This is more about the experience, rather than the quality. Buy a *majlis* setting here. ⊗ Map N1 • Mina (Port) Rd

### 6 Fotouh Al Khair Centre
Expats love this bright mini mall. It is home to Marks and Spencer (with a small but really good food hall), Monsoon and other popular UK brands. ⊗ Map P3 • Near Etisalat, opposite Cultural Foundation • 02 621 1133

### 7 Khalifa Centre
Bargain for exquisite Persian rugs, sheeshas, tribal kilims or even silver prayer holders. ⊗ Map P1 • Tenth St, opp Abu Dhabi Mall, Tourist Club area • 02 667 9900

### 8 Hamdan St
This local "high street" sells everything. It has jewellery stores, Arabic and Bollywood music shops as well as discount supermarkets. ⊗ Map P3 • Sheikh Hamdan bin Mohammed St (Hamdan St)

### 9 THE One
See how Abu Dhabi's expats decorate their flash apartments at this contemporary furniture and interior design store. They also have candles, photo frames, gifts and CDs. ⊗ Map P5 • BMW Showroom, Khalidiya • 02 681 0229

### 10 Liwa Centre
Better for people-watching than actual shopping these days, Liwa is the place to shop (along with Hamdan Centre next door) for cheap clothes, jewellery, glasses, accessories, souvenirs and mobile phones. ⊗ Map P3 • Near Novotel Hotel, Hamdan St • 02 632 0344

**Price Categories**

| | | |
|---|---|---|
| For a three-course meal for one with half a bottle of wine (or equivalent meal), taxes and extra charges. | **D** | Under AED 25 |
| | **DD** | AED 25–100 |
| | **DDD** | AED 100–150 |
| | **DDDD** | AED 150–250 |
| | **DDDDD** | Over AED 250 |

Left **Deck tables at Finz's beach shack** Right **A belly dancer performing at Marrakesh**

# Restaurants

### Bord Eau

This elegant French restaurant in the Shangri-La Qaryat Al Beri hotel *(see p116)* offers classic French dishes and also modern, innovative cuisine. There is an excellent wine list. 🌐 *Shangri-La Hotel, Qaryat Al Beri • 02 509 8888 • Open 7pm–11:30pm • DDDDD*

### Embassy

The Michelin-starred chef at this glamorous restaurant in the Emirates Palace hotel *(see pp22–23)* has created a superb menu using classic ingredients. 🌐 *Map N6 • Emirates Palace Hotel, Corniche West • 02 690 8888 • Open 7pm–11:30pm Tue –Sun • DDDDD*

### Sayad

Don't let the blue lighting and playful decor distract you too much from the fine seafood cuisine on offer at this swanky restaurant. 🌐 *Map N6 • Emirates Palace Hotel, Corniche West • 02 690 8888 • Open 7:30pm–midnight • DDDDD*

### Jazz Bar

Creative cuisine served in two sizes – "downbeat" for light eaters and "main melody" for the hungry! 🌐 *Map P6 • Hilton Abu Dhabi, Corniche Rd West • 02 681 1900 • Open 7:30pm–1:30am • DDDD*

### Shang Palace

Chinese cuisine cooked with panache and expertise. 🌐 *Shangri-La Hotel, Qaryat Al Beri • 02 509 8888 • Open noon–3pm & 7pm–11:30pm • DDDD*

### Finz

This chic beach shack serves food in a nautical setting. 🌐 *Map Q1 • Beach Rotana Hotel, Tourist Club area • 02 644 3000 • Open noon–3pm & 7pm–midnight • DDDD*

### Trader Vic's

An Abu Dhabi institution, this Polynesian restaurant was once the city's best and still holds a special place in people's hearts and stomachs. 🌐 *Map Q1 • Beach Rotana Hotel, Tourist Club area • 02 644 3000 • Open noon–3pm & 7pm–midnight • DDDD*

### Prego's

Sit on the terrace and enjoy delicious olive tapenade, hot breads and wood-fired pizzas. 🌐 *Map Q1 • Beach Rotana Hotel, Tourist Club area • 02 644 3000 • Open noon–midnight • DDD*

### Amalfi

Popular with business people, this elegant restaurant serves up well-executed Italian cuisine in plush surroundings. 🌐 *Map N2 • Le Royal Meridien, Khalifa St • 02 695 0583 • Open noon–3pm & 7pm–midnight • DDD*

### Marrakesh

Savour authentic Moroccan cuisine at this opulent restaurant, while enjoying the belly dancer and Moroccan band. Try the succulent chicken lemon tajine. 🌐 *Map P2 • Millennium Hotel, Khalifa St • 02 626 2700 • Open 7pm–2am • DDDD*

*If bread and butter or olive oil are served at a restaurant, you can trust they'll be complimentary, but not so with water.*

Left **Soba's heavenly sashimi** Centre **Chefs at Lebanese Flower** Right **A lit-up India Palace**

# Cheap Global Eats

### 1 Zen
Settle down at the sushi counter for some sashimi or visit the teppanyaki bar for some BBQ action. ✪ *Map N2 • Al Ain Palace Hotel, Corniche East • 02 79 4112 • Open noon–3pm & 7:30pm–midnight • DDD*

### 2 Taste of Thailand
Be prepared for a traditional Thai greeting and delicious Thai favourites. ✪ *Map N2 • Al Ain Palace Hotel, Corniche East • 02 679 4777 • Open noon–3pm & 7pm–11pm • DDD*

### 3 Shamyat
You'll love the Syrian food, vine-covered ceiling and ladies baking traditional bread over a fire. ✪ *Map N1 • Al Salam St, near Al Diar Regency Hotel • 02 671 2600 • Open 11am–midnight • DD; no alcohol*

### 4 Pars Palace
Feast on exceptional Persian cuisine. Try the saffron rice with pomegranate seeds and kebabs with rich sauces. ✪ *Map P4 • Al Araby St, Khalidiya, behind Corniche Towers • 02 681 8600 • Open 1am–3:30pm & 6pm–midnight • DD; no alcohol*

### 5 Soba
This sushi bar is ideal for a fast eat. The chefs are fun to watch and there's a DJ after 9pm. ✪ *Map N2 • Le Royal Meridien Hotel, Khalifa St • 02 695 0450 • Open 1pm–3:30pm & 7pm–10:30pm • DDD*

### 6 Royal Orchid
You'll be lured in by the fish tank under the floor and great Thai staples. ✪ *Map P6 • Al Salam St • 02 644 4400 / 644 1100 • Open noon–3pm & 6pm–midnight • DD; no alcohol*

### 7 India Palace
Dine on North Indian cuisine in an opulent Raj decor. ✪ *Map P1 • Al Salam St • 02 644 8777 • Open noon–3pm & 6pm–midnight • DD; no alcohol*

### 8 Lebanese Flower
A must-visit for scrumptious *mezze* (Arabic appetizers such as hommous and vine leaves), smoky mixed grilled meat plates, honey-soaked *baklava* and Turkish coffee. ✪ *Map P3 • Near Choitrams Supermarket, cnr Hamdan & Fourth St, Khalidya • 02 665 8700 / 666 6888 • Open 10am–2am • DD; no alcohol*

### 9 Automatic
Grab a delicious chicken and garlic *shwarma* sandwich and a thick mango juice at this popular joint. ✪ *Map P2 • Cnr Hamdan & Najda St • 02 677 2412 • Open 11am–1am • D; no alcohol*

### 10 Arab Udupi
This popular branch of this chain of cheap Pakistani eateries dishes up saucy meat curries to a mixed crowd of expats. ✪ *Map P2 • Behind BHS, off Hamdan St • 02 677 4307 • Open 24 hours • D; no alcohol*

**Price Categories**

For a three-course meal for one with half a bottle of wine (or equivalent meal), taxes and extra charges.

| | |
|---|---|
| **D** | Under AED 25 |
| **DD** | AED 25–100 |
| **DDD** | AED 100–150 |
| **DDDD** | AED 150–250 |
| **DDDDD** | Over AED 250 |

Left **Zari Zardozi's exotic setting** Right **A cocktail maker in action at Trader Vic's**

# Bars & Clubs

### 1 Cristal Cigar & Champagne Bar

For a sophisticated evening, stop by this "gentlemen's club" style bar for a glass of bubbly. ◎ *Map P2 • Millennium Hotel, Khalifa St • 02 626 2700 • Open 4pm–2am*

### 2 Jazz Bar

Enjoy live jazz as you dine or simply have a drink at this Art Deco inspired bar *(see p93)*.

### 3 Sax

Dance to live improvisational music on Tuesday's boisterous Lebanese night at this swanky bar-club. Book in advance. ◎ *Map N2 • Le Royal Meridien Abu Dhabi • 02 674 2020 / 674 1286 • Open 7pm–2:30am*

### 4 Al Fanar

Enjoy the views while sipping a cocktail at this revolving rooftop restaurant and bar. ◎ *Map N2 • Le Royal Meridien • 02 695 0583 • Open 12:30pm–3pm all days; 7pm–11pm Fri–Wed & 7pm–midnight Thu*

### 5 Trader Vic's Bar

Kickstart the night with a lethal cocktail – in a big glass with umbrellas – at this Polynesian-themed bar and restaurant *(see p93)*.

### 6 Oceans

Chill out on big white cushions on high-backed cane sofas at this breezy lounge bar. If it is too hot outside, head in to the cool colonial style interior. ◎ *Map N2 • Le Royal Meridien, Khalifa St • 02 674 1094 • Open noon–1:30am*

### 7 Embassy

This exclusive restaurant, bar, lounge and members club is the first of its kind in Abu Dhabi. It is becoming the place to be seen *(see p93)*.

### 8 Zari Zardozi

Enjoy DJs spinning Indian fusion, live music and even a belly dancer at this big, exotic Indian hotspot *(see p93)*.

### 9 Zenith

This intimate dance club has a space-age circular dance floor with flashing square lights and swanky leather seats in prime people-watching position. ◎ *Map N1 • Sheraton Abu Dhabi Resort & Towers Hotel, Corniche • 02 677 3333 • Open 9pm–2:30am Wed–Sat*

### 10 Colosseum

With different DJs every night, the city's oldest dance club is in a cavernous space with a sunken dance floor, a conversation bar upstairs and VIP area behind the DJ. ◎ *Map P1 • Abu Dhabi Marina, Tourist Club area • 02 644 0300 • Open 9pm–4am Tue–Sun*

Left **P J O'Reilly's Irish pub** Centre **The 49ers horseshoe emblem** Right **Brauhaus' German brews**

# TOP 10 Expat Pubs

### 1 Hemingways
The stale beer smell and smoke is part of this popular institution's attraction. ✎ *Map P6 • Hilton Abu Dhabi Hotel, Corniche West • 02 681 1900 • Open noon–midnight*

### 2 Brauhaus
Have a German beer with old-timers on a lazy afternoon. ✎ *Map Q1 • Beach Rotana Hotel, Tourist Club area • 02 644 3000 • Open 4pm–1am*

### 3 Heroes
Great table service ensures you'll always get a drink at this sports bar, no matter how packed it is. ✎ *Map P2 • Crowne Plaza Hotel, Sheikh Hamdan bin Mohammed St • 02 621 0000 • Open noon–2:30am*

### 4 P J O'Reilly's
This Irish pub keeps everyone happy with its "pub grub" and friendly staff. ✎ *Map N2 • Le Royal Meridien, Khalifa St • 02 695 0515 • Open noon–3am*

### 5 Captain's Arms
Get cosy inside this traditional English pub or lounge on its sunny garden outside. ✎ *Map P1 • Le Meridien Abu Dhabi, Tourist Club area • 02 644 6666 • Open noon–midnight*

### 6 The Harvester's Pub
You'll see a rowdy crowd leaving their dartboards to enjoy an on-screen match at this smoky basement bar. Try the bangers and mash. ✎ *Map P2 • Al Diar Sands Hotel, Zayed the First St • 02 633 5335 / 615 6666 • Open noon–2am*

### 7 Regent's Pub
This endearingly old-fashioned English pub has a largely British expat crowd. The beers here are cheap. ✎ *Map N1 • Al Diar Regency Hotel, Mina Rd • 02 676 5000 • Open 5pm–2am*

### 8 49ers
Head here early as this pub, subtitled "the Gold Rush", gets packed, particularly when there's a band on. ✎ *Map P2 • Al Diar Dana Hotel, Zayed the First St • 02 645 8000 • Open noon–2:30am*

### 9 Rock Bottom Café
The big juicy steaks, good live music, a boisterous atmosphere and discounted beverages will keep you coming back for more. ✎ *Map P1 • Al Diar Capital Hotel, Hamdan Bin Mohammed St • 02 677 7655 • Open noon–2am*

### 10 Ally Pally Corner
Head to this typical English pub for Guinness and to hear Gulf war stories and tales of pre-oil times from the city's older expat males. ✎ *Map N2 • Al Ain Palace Hotel, The Corniche East • 02 679 4777 • Open noon–1:30am*

Left **Marina Mall** Centre **Hitting the Corniche for a walk** Right **Emirates Palace's opulent interiors**

# ₁₀ Best of the Rest

### Corniche walk
Pack your walking shoes and schedule your saunter down Abu Dhabi's splendid Corniche for the late afternoon so you won't miss the spectacular sunsets *(see pp88–91).*

### Hamdan Street
Bustling neon-lit Hamdan Street doesn't have the stylish shops of the swish shopping malls but its vibrant atmosphere, best appreciated at night, make it a more interesting place to shop *(see p92).*

### Go shopping
Laidback Abu Dhabi is a more relaxing place to shop than Dubai and the air-conditioned malls provide relief from the heat. Evenings are best, when local Emiratis love to shop.

### Emirates Palace tour
Not staying at this opulent hotel? Then a tour is a must. You can explore yourself but a guided tour ensures you don't miss a single detail and includes afternoon tea *(see pp22–3).*

### Palace drive
Take a taxi or hire a car to explore impressive Al Bateen neighbourhood. The colossal Sheikhs' palaces, their high walls, verdant gardens and armoured vehicles make for a memorable experience. ✆ *Map Q5 • Al Bateen area • Taxi AED20, hire car from AED150 per day*

### City skyline view
Spectacular views of the city's Manhattan-like skyline can be enjoyed from the big flag pole at the end of the Breakwater *(see pp88–91).*

### Cruise
The stunning Corniche and Abu Dhabi skyline are best appreciated from the sea. Savour the fresh seafood and sparkling city views from Le Royal Meridien's sleek Shuja Yacht on a cruise. ✆ *Map N5 • Departs from the Marina at The Broadwater • 02 695 0539 • Times vary: sunset and dinner cruises (8pm–10:30pm) • Adm*

### Sunset drinks at Al Fanar
Enjoy a bird's eye view of this stunning city of skyscrapers as you sip a cocktail and watch the sun set from this stylish revolving restaurant *(see p95).*

### Ghantoot Racing & Polo Club
Watch Emirati and Argentine polo teams practice or play an exciting match on sprawling landscaped lawns. ✆ *Ghantoot Racing & Polo Club, Dubai-Abu Dhabi Rd • 02 562 9050 • Nov–Apr*

### Dine at Jazz Bar
Enjoy an exquisite meal while listening to fabulous live jazz – often performed by excellent South African bands – at this Abu Dhabi institution. Book in advance for weekends *(see p92).*

# STREETSMART

DUBAI & ABU DHABI'S TOP 10

Left **A sunny day at the beach** Right **Deira City Centre mall**

# Planning Your Trip

### 1 Passports & Visa
Complimentary 60-day visit visas are available on arrival at UAE airport immigration desks. Passports must be valid for 6 months from the date of entry to the UAE. Visas can be extended at the Department of Naturalisation and Residency (Tel: 02 398 1010). 🔍 *Visa free; visa extension Dh500 for 30 days • dxbimmig@emirates.net.ae • www.dnrd.gov.ae*

### 2 Insurance
While petty crime is extremely rare in the UAE, insurance covering loss of luggage and theft is always good to have, along with comprehensive health and dental insurance. Hospitals are very efficient, but the services are expensive.

### 3 When to Go
Winter is usually when Dubai is at its best. This is when the Dubai Shopping Festival, Global Village and most major international sporting events take place. In recent years though, the UAE has had cool, grey, wet winters. So those wanting guaranteed sunshine should visit during Oct–Nov or Mar–Apr instead. Summer is best avoided.

### 4 What to Take
Bring swimwear, a hat and sun block (expensive in the UAE) for the beach. Loose linen and cotton clothes are best for sightseeing. Make sure they're not transparent – remember, it's a conservative country, so you need to dress modestly. Pack a cardigan or sweater as most indoor places are air-conditioned.

### 5 How Long to Stay
While Dubai makes a great 2–3 day stopover on your way somewhere, 5 days to a week is wonderful if you want to relax at a beach resort, do some serious shopping in the souqs and malls, as well as take in the sights of Dubai Creek, Bastakiya and Shindagha. Add 1–2 days to visit Abu Dhabi.

### 6 Electricity
UAE power sockets generally accept the UK three prong plug operating on 220/240 volts, although you may also see the European two round prong plug. It's not a bad idea to bring an adaptor that works for both. Most good hotels will have adaptors you can borrow, or you can buy them in local supermarkets.

### 7 Customs & Duty Free
The duty free allowance is 400 cigarettes or 2 kg of tobacco, cigars to the value of AED 3000 and 5 litres of wine or spirits. It's illegal to purchase alcohol in the UAE without a liquor license (only available to UAE Residents), so buy duty free at the airport if you want to have sunset drinks on the balcony but want to avoid expensive mini-bar costs.

### 8 Prohibited Items
In addition to the items on most countries' blacklists, such as firearms, illegal drugs and pornography, it is forbidden to bring in any banned movies, tv programs and offensive publications, especially films and programs that may include scenes with passionate kissing, sex, nudity or semi-nudity, drug-use or any content relating to Israel.

### 9 Time Zone
The UAE time zone is GMT+4. It is 6 hours behind Australian Eastern Standard Time. There is no daylight saving.

### 10 Opening Hours & Weekends
The UAE weekend is Friday and Saturday. Business hours aren't fixed, but generally, shopping malls open 10am–10pm Sat–Thu, opening in the late afternoon and evening on Fridays. Shops in the streets open approximately the same times but close for lunch from 1pm–4/5pm. Government departments open around 7am and close to the public around 3pm.

➡ *Dubai has several good local English-language TV stations. Most hotel rooms feature global satellite channels like CNN and BBC.*

Left **An Emirates Airlines flight** Centre **Local papers & magazines** Right **Dubai Visitor Info logo**

# 🔟 Travel Information Sources

### 1 UAE Interact
The excellent website of the UAE Ministry for Information and Culture is easy to use. It covers everything you need to know about the UAE from daily news and useful information to fascinating articles on aspects of Emirati culture, with downloadable annual reports and short videos. ✆ www.uaeinteract.com

### 2 UAE Federal e-Government Portal
This outstanding website not only provides information on the UAE and its government, but also helpful information to travellers about visas, passports, customs, transport and telecommunications information and links. ✆ www.uae.gov.ae

### 3 Dubai Tourism & Commerce Marketing
Look here for a wide range of information for travellers, from destination content and accommodation listings, to more interesting coverage on local culture, sights, shopping and other things to do. ✆ www.dubaitourism.ae

### 4 Sheikh Mohammed's Website
The fascinating website of the visionary UAE Prime Minister and Ruler of Dubai, Sheikh Mohammed bin Rashid Al Maktoum, has comprehensive information on the UAE, as well as sections featuring the Sheikh's poetry and wisdom. The website lets you to write an email to the Sheikh and receive a royal response! ✆ www.sheikhmohammed.com

### 5 UAE Airlines
Access destination information, check timetables, book flights online or even hire a car, on the websites of UAE's airlines – Etihad Airline (www.etihad.com), Emirates Airline (www.emirates.com) and budget airline Air Arabia (www.airarabia.com).

### 6 Emirates News Agency (WAM)
Spend some time trawling through the news releases on this site. You'll dig up everything from which world leader the UAE President sent a telegram to that day, to the changes to property laws. ✆ www.wam.org.ae

### 7 Media
The UAE has a number of dreadful newspapers which print government press releases word for word. Much more interesting are the free newspapers, Seven Days and Emirates Today, which focus on UAE content. ✆ Dh2 for most newspapers

### 8 Entertainment Media
Time Out Dubai and Time Out Abu Dhabi magazines include comprehensive listings for arts and cultural events, restaurants, bars, clubs and sporting activities. The Time Out website is also a great source of information so you can plan and buy tickets to big events online. Expat-focused What's On magazine is also good. ✆ AED 5 for Time Out magazine • www.timeoutdubai.com; www.timeoutabudhabi.com; www.timeouttickets.com

### 9 Dubai Tourism Info Centre
If sightseeing along Deira Creek or shopping in the souqs, head to the main tourism office on Baniyas Square, in a traditional-looking windtower building, for information. Temporarily sealed off while construction of the new Baniyas Station takes place, it's due to re-open in 2008. ✆ Map L2 • Baniyas Square, Deira • Open 9am–9pm Sat–Thu, 3pm–9pm Fri • www.dubaitourism.ae

### 10 Dubai Tourism Visitor Information Bureaus
You'll find helpful Visitor Information Bureaus at the airport and all major shopping malls. ✆ Dubai Airport: 04 224 5252 • Open 24 hours • www.dubaitourism.au

> You'll find the excellent complimentary Concierge and Visitor magazines in most five star hotel rooms.

Left **The Abu Dhabi Airport terminal** Right **Abu Dhabi's Al Ghazal taxi**

# 🔟 Arriving in Dubai & Abu Dhabi

### 1 Dubai International Airport

Sleek Dubai Airport is one of the world's best. Good signage directs passengers to Arrivals. The Emirati staff are efficient. If you're from one of the 34 countries eligible for an on-the-spot visa, the process is a breeze. 🕾 04 224 5555 • www.dubaiairport.com

### 2 Abu Dhabi International Airport

All planes pull into Abu Dhabi airport's attractive mushroom-shaped satellite, so you don't have far to walk to Immigration and the baggage carousel beyond. Service is efficient, and if you come from one of the 34 countries eligible for visas on arrival, the process is quick. 🕾 02 575 7500 • www.dcaauh. gov.ae

### 3 Marhaba & Golden Class Services

To enjoy five star service or for special assistance, organize to be met by the Marhaba Service in Dubai or Golden Class in Abu Dhabi. For a fee, a hostess greets you on arrival, whisks you through a special immigration line, helps you with your luggage, and escorts you to your transport. 🕾 Golden Class, Abu Dhabi: 02 575 7466 • Marhaba Service, Dubai: 04 224 5780

### 4 Immigration

One way to help immigration procedures go smoothly is to greet officials in Arabic. Try "As'salam Alaykum" ("Peace be upon you") to which they should warmly respond: "Wa'alaykum salaam" (literally meaning "and peace right back to you"). If you don't come from a country eligible for an on-the-spot visa, make sure you have your UAE embassy-issued visa documents.

### 5 Duty-Free & Customs

There are duty-free shops at Arrivals at Dubai and Abu Dhabi airports. After collecting your luggage choose the "Nothing to Declare" or "Declare" exit. Customs officers randomly select passengers to put their luggage through the X-ray machine again or occasionally ask you to open your bags. 🕾 www. auhcustoms.gov.ae

### 6 Arrivals Hall

Once through Customs, you'll come to the Arrivals Hall, which is jam-packed with desks representing tourism agencies, car rental companies, hotel desks, an accommodation booking service, ATMs and mobile phone retailers. It would be a good idea to get some cash from the ATM here for the taxi to your hotel.

### 7 Dubai Airport Taxis

It isn't difficult to find a taxi at Dubai's airport. The flag fall is AED 20 from the airport. The fare into Deira is around AED 35, to Bur Dubai AED 35–45 and to Jumeirah AED 55–75. 🕾 Dubai Transport • 04 208 0808, 286 1616, 227 3840 • www.dtc.dubai.ae

### 8 Abu Dhabi Airport Taxis

The Al Ghazal taxis outside Abu Dhabi's airport ferry you to the city centre for around AED 65–75. For a limousine to the city centre for AED 65, book through Golden Class. 🕾 Al Ghazal: 02 444 7787; Golden Class: 02 575 7466

### 9 Dubai Airport Bus

Budget travellers can use the convenient Airport Bus Service. The 401 goes to Union Square, Baniyas Rd, Al-Sabkha bus station and Deira bus station. The 402 travels via Deira City Centre to Karama, Mankhool and Bur Dubai. Both cost around AED 3.

### 10 Abu Dhabi Airport Bus

There is currently no Airport Bus service from Abu Dhabi Airport into the city centre. However, it is rumoured that Abu Dhabi municipality has plans to start one. For updates on this, travellers should call 02 443 1500.

*Taxis can be reluctant to hand over change. Leave a few coins if the driver has helped you with your luggage and been courteous.*

Left **An *abra* ride** Right **A local bus**

# 🔟 Getting Around

### 1 Car Rental
There are car rental desks in the Arrivals halls of the airports and also at most hotels. Europcar offers the best prices as well as a drop-off and pick-up service. ◈ *Europcar: Abu Dhabi 02 626 1441; Dubai 04 224 5240 • Thrifty: Abu Dhabi 02 575 7400; Dubai 04 800 4694 • Budget: Abu Dhabi 02 633 4200; Dubai 04 295 6667*

### 2 Driving Conditions & Road Rules
Only the brave drive in the UAE, which has one of the highest road death rates in the world. Drive on the right side of the road. Unless otherwise sign-posted, speed limits are 60km/h on city streets, 80km/h on major city roads, 100–120km/h on highways. Do not drink and drive. There is a zero-tolerance policy – if caught, you're sure to spend the night in jail.

### 3 Dubai Taxis
There are taxi ranks at shopping malls. Elsewhere, flag them down on the street. All taxis use metres. The flag fall is AED 3 by day, AED 3.50 at night. A short taxi ride in Deira or Bur Dubai might cost you AED 10, from Deira to Sheikh Zayed Rd around AED 15, from Bur Dubai to Jumeirah Beach from AED 25–45. ◈ *Dubai Transport: 04 208 0808 • www.dtc.dubai.ae*

### 4 Abu Dhabi Taxis
Regular taxis are cheap in Abu Dhabi. A short ride in the city will cost from AED 3–15. Flag taxis down on the street. During peak times from 8am–9am and 5pm–6pm, weekend evenings and prayer times, when it's impossible to find a taxi, phone ahead and book one through the upmarket but expensive Al Ghazal service.

### 5 Dubai Bus Service
The bus service has 62 routes around Dubai. Details of routes are available on the Roads and Transport Authority's (RTA) website www.rta.ae. It includes a helpful "journey planner". Fares range from AED 1–3. ◈ *04 800 90 90 (Open 24 hours)*

### 6 Inter-Emirate Bus Service
The RTA also runs a bus service to other emirates. Frequent services operate from 6am to midnight daily from bus stations in Deira (for northern emirates) and Bur Dubai (to Abu Dhabi and Al Ain).

### 7 Long Distance Taxis
There are long distance shared taxi services from Dubai and Abu Dhabi bus stations to all emirates. Taxis leave when they're full. Fares are similar to the buses but taxis are faster. Not all have air-conditioning and they can get cramped. Dubai Transport operates a shared taxi to Abu Dhabi for AED 50. ◈ *Dubai Transport: 04 208 0808*

### 8 Al Ghazal Service
Abu Dhabi's Al Ghazal taxis can drive you to other emirates and provide a door-to-door service. Book at least an hour ahead. The fare from Abu Dhabi to Dubai is AED 275. The return trip is AED 175. ◈ *Al Ghazal 02 444 7787*

### 9 Abras
The *abras* continually criss-cross Dubai Creek connecting Deira and Bur Dubai from 5am to midnight daily. The fare is AED 1 per person. You can hire your own *abra* to cruise the Creek for AED 100 an hour. Docks are handily situated at Bur Dubai Souq, Deira Spice Souq, Al Sabkha, Al Seef Park and Dubai Municipality. ◈ *04 800 9090*

### 10 Walking
There are few places that are walkable in Dubai and Abu Dhabi, apart from Dubai's souqs and Bastakiya and Abu Dhabi's Corniche. Elsewhere, be cautious on pedestrian crossings, which drivers ignore. Walking is better in the cooler winter months. However, in the scorching heat of summer, it's not advisable as there is little shelter.

*A ride on an abra across bustling Dubai Creek is for many a highlight of a trip to Dubai – make sure you do it at least once!*

Left **An exchange centre sign** Centre **An Emirates Post mail box** Right **A prepaid phone card**

# Banking & Communications

### Currency
The UAE's currency is the UAE dirham, written as AED (Arab Emirates Dirham) or as Dh. One dirham is divided into 100 fils. Notes are in denominations of AED 5, AED 10, AED 20, AED 50, AED 100, AED 200, AED 500 and AED 1000. Coins are available as 25 fils, 50 fils as well as one dirham.

### Exchange Rates
The UAE dirham is pegged to the US dollar. US$ 1 is equal to AED 3.67. All other currencies fluctuate, but at the time of writing Euro 1 was equal to AED 4.6 and GBP 1 was worth AED 7.

### Banks & ATMs
Numerous international banks operate in the UAE, including HSBC, Citibank and Standard Chartered Bank. Good local banks include National Bank of Abu Dhabi, Mashreq Bank and National Bank of Dubai. Globally linked ATMs are everywhere, allowing you access to your home account.

### Credit Cards & Travellers' Cheques
While travellers' cheques can be changed in the UAE, credit cards are preferred. Visa, American Express and Mastercard are widely accepted and credit cards can be used almost everywhere. If using travellers' cheques, opt for Thomas Cook, which has local branches.

### Calling the UAE
To phone the UAE from abroad, dial your international access code, the UAE country code 971, then 4 for Dubai or 2 for Abu Dhabi, followed by the local number. To dial a mobile from abroad, dial 971 50 followed by the mobile number. Within the UAE, dial 050 for mobiles, 04 to call Dubai from outside the emirate and 02 to phone Abu Dhabi from another emirate.

### Mobile Phones
Etisalat is the national telecommunications company. Etisalat's excellent "Ahlan: Visitors Mobile Package" for cell phones costs AED 90, lasts 90 days and is available at the Etisalat kiosks, grocery stores, petrol stations and street kiosks. ◉ www.etisalat.ae

### Phone Cards
Buy an AED 20 Pre-Paid Card to make calls from public phones in the UAE, to make calls to the UAE from other countries and to pay for WI-FI internet services at Etisalat iZone Hot Spots. ◉ www.etisalat.ae

### Internet Access
Etisalat's wireless internet (WI-FI) service can be accessed at iZone Hotspots at airports, shopping malls, coffee shops, restaurants and business centres. A prepaid card costs AED 15 an hour, AED 30 for 3 hours, AED 70 for 24 hours or AED 120 for a 60-day stay. Internet cafés are widely available in the cities.

### Post Offices
Emirates Post is the UAE's national postal service. You can buy stamps at any post office and at some stationery shops. Mail to Europe, North America and Australasia takes about 10 days. It's unreliable, however, so register anything valuable or use a courier for anything urgent. ◉ Dubai Main Post Office: 04 262 2222 • Abu Dhabi Central Post Office: 02 621 1611 • Main post offices: Open 8am–10pm Sat–Thu, 8am–noon Fri • www.emiratespost.co.ae

### Shipping & Couriers
Emirates Post provides surface and air delivery services for sending large parcels. See their website for details. Courier services are more reliable. Companies with a good reputation for service include Aramex, FedEx and DHL. All will pick-up from your hotel – you can pay on pick-up if you don't have an account. ◉ Aramex: 04 286 5000 • FedEx: 800 4050 • DHL: 800 4004 • www.emiratespost.co.ae

Left **An Emirati woman** Centre **A local mosque** Right **A session of "Open Doors, Open Minds"**

# 🔟 Things to be Aware of

### 1 Languages
Arabic is the official language, although English is widely spoken. As 80% of the population are foreign, you'll hear scores of languages on the street. Signage is generally in both Arabic and English.

### 2 Islam
The UAE is an Islamic state following a tolerant version of Sharia Law, with both Sharia and civil law courts. UAE Muslims adhere to the conduct of Islam, praying five times a day, donating to charity, fasting and doing the pilgrimage to Mecca.

### 3 Call-to-prayer
If you stay in Deira, Bur Dubai or the Bastakiya area in particular, you'll hear the beautiful sound of the call-to-prayer echoing through the streets five times a day. Broadcast from the minarets of mosques, the call-to-prayer beckons Muslims to come and worship.

### 4 Respectful Conduct
Never shake hands with an Emirati woman unless offered her hand first. If visiting someone's home, remove your shoes, don't show the soles of your feet and don't eat with your left hand. Displays of affection among couples in public are frowned upon. While holding hands is acceptable, passionate kissing and embracing is not. Rude gestures and swearing are offensive.

### 5 Photographing Women
Photographing Emirati and other Muslim women is not acceptable without asking their permission first. Even at places where covered ladies prepare local food for sale as part of the displays, ask first before taking their photo. Photography of Sheikhs' palaces, police and military buildings, ports and airports is forbidden.

### 6 Dress Code
Visitors should dress modestly. Loose long linen or cotton clothing is respectful and is also suited to the scorching heat. Women should not wear tight or transparent clothing, skirts above the knee, sleeveless tops, halter-necks or shoestring straps in public, while men should refrain from wearing shorts and sleeveless tops. In Sharjah, wearing these clothes in public can incur a severe penalty.

### 7 Pork
Muslims do not eat pork, however, pork products are for sale to non-Muslims in "Pork Rooms" in supermarkets such as Spinneys. Most restaurants at five star hotels include pork on their menus.

### 8 Alcohol
It's illegal to purchase alcohol without a liquor license (only available to UAE Residents) so buy alcohol at the airport duty free shop. You can drink alcohol in hotels and licensed venues. Penalties for drunken behaviour in public are heavy. Sharjah is a dry emirate – alcohol is not sold or allowed there.

### 9 Sheikh Mohammed Centre for Cultural Understanding
This organization runs a number of activities under the "Open Doors, Open Minds" program, which is aimed at promoting tolerance of culture and religion. Stop at the Bastakiya court-yard house to book a tour (see pp12–13).

### 10 Ramadan & Islamic holidays
Religious festivals rely on the sighting of the moon. Alcohol is not served the night before a religious holiday. During the holy month of Ramadan, government offices operate on shorter hours, most shops close during the day, and eating, drinking and smoking in public is forbidden. There is no music or dancing either. After *Iftar* (breaking of the fast), the mood is festive – malls stay open until midnight and the celebratory spirit is infectious.

Left **Soft drink vending machines** Centre **"Camel Crossing" road sign** Right **A beach warning**

# 🔟 Things to Avoid

### 1 Dehydration
Whether lying by the pool or walking around town, you're equally at risk of dehydrating in the UAE's ferocious heat. To avoid dehydration, wear light clothes, avoid the sun in the hottest part of the day and drink much more water than you normally would at home.

### 2 Traffic Accidents
Dubai's traffic is horrific. Be vigilant as a pedestrian and as a passenger don't be embarrassed to ask your driver to "*shway shway!*" (slow down!).

### 3 Rush Hour
Don't think about going anywhere in Dubai from 8am–10am (when commuters head to work), noon–2pm (when they go home or out for lunch) and from 4pm–6:30pm. Also avoid the roads around 8pm–9pm on Thursday and Friday nights, when everyone seems to be going out.

### 4 Parking & Speeding Tickets
UAE parking and traffic cops take their jobs very seriously. Look out for speed signs, particularly in areas where there are road works. Always look for parking signs and orange parking metres wherever you park, especially at night. Otherwise, expect to return to a parking ticket on your windscreen.

### 5 Road Surprises!
While you might find those "Road Surprises!" signs amusing the first time you see them (and everyone loves to stop to take a photo of the camel sign), they're there for a reason. Slow down and look out for dips, speed bumps and sand on the road. And while they're very cute, camels can be troublesome – they just love to take a stroll on the freeway.

### 6 Driving in Rain & Sand Storms
Rainy weather makes driving hazardous simply because UAE residents aren't used to driving in the rain, so they won't necessarily slow down. The rate of accidents is considerably higher in wet weather. Decelerate or pull over in sand storms when visibility is poor. When you see oncoming drivers with their hazard lights on, it means conditions are even worse up ahead.

### 7 Swimming Dangers
When you see signs warning bathers about dangerous rips and strong undertows, these should be taken seriously. Avoid swimming if you're not a strong swimmer, or take extra care. Despite the calm appearance of the water, Dubai's beaches have very powerful undercurrents.

### 8 Souq Spruikers
The most annoying thing about shopping in the souqs is the spruiking. Touts aggressively attempt to lure customers into shops to buy "copy watches, copy bags, Madam!" Unless you want to buy these counterfeit goods (great value but illegal), the best strategy is to ignore them completely. Show even the slightest bit of interest or politeness, and they'll never leave you alone.

### 9 Drugs
Do not attempt to bring drugs into the country. Keep in mind that even some prescription drugs, such as codeine, are banned. The UAE has a zero tolerance policy on drugs. Penalties and sentences are harsh. While the death penalty is an option, it's rarely applied. However, you're more likely to serve a long sentence and get deported.

### 10 Prostitutes
If you stay in Bur Dubai neighbourhoods such as Mankhool, you'll see prostitutes on the streets at night, often from China and former Soviet countries. They also frequent many bars and nightclubs in Deira and Bur Dubai. Prostitution is illegal and prostitutes are best avoided.

Left **Year-round sunshine at Dubai beaches** Right **Signs for public conveniences**

# 🔟 Useful Information

## 1 Business & Shopping Hours

The official weekend is Friday and Saturday. Everyone has a day off on the main Friday prayer day, while some work half or full days on Saturday. Government departments open 7:30am–3pm while private companies work 9am–5pm. Supermarkets open 8am–10pm while major malls open 10am–10pm. Smaller malls and independent shops do not open until the afternoon on Fridays.

## 2 Climate

The UAE has an arid sub-tropical climate with infrequent rainfall. The country was synonymous with year-round sunshine until the 2006 winter, one of the wettest on record. Temperatures average 20 degrees Celsius in winter to 45 degrees Celsius in summer.

## 3 Weights & Measures

The UAE uses the metric system, except for petrol, when it uses gallons. A wide range of measurement systems are used for clothes and shoes which are manufactured in Europe, Asia, the Middle East and North America.

## 4 Taxes

Residents of the UAE don't pay income tax. This is a big incentive for expats to build a life here. The only taxes here are on alcohol and the municipality and service taxes on hotel rooms.

## 5 Photography & Video

Emiratis are obsessed with technology so if you're after something new you'll find a wide range of well-priced digital cameras. If you need additional memory cards, tapes or batteries try the myriad electronics stores in City Centre and Baniyas Square, Deira.

## 6 Smoking

UAE legislation introduced in 2004 provided for a ban on smoking in public places, including shopping malls, restaurants and entertainment venues. Unfortunately this has not been enforced. By law, restaurants are required to have non-smoking sections but most don't. At the time of research the UAE was set to enforce laws and give officials power to issue on-the-spot fines to lawbreakers.

## 7 Homosexuality

Homosexuality is illegal and homosexual practices are punishable with harsh penalties. You'll see men from Central Asia and the Indian Subcontinent holding hands – this does not mean they are gay; they are just good friends. Likewise, you'll see Emirati men rub noses when they meet, in the same way that close male friends kiss cheeks in Europe's Mediterranean countries.

## 8 Women Travellers

Women travelling solo in the UAE shouldn't experience any harassment if they follow local norms. They should sit in the back seat of taxis, in the "women's section" of buses and eat in "family rooms" in cheap hotels. Dedicated women's queues at banks and government departments mean women get preferential service.

## 9 Contraceptives

Contraceptives can be purchased in pharmacies in the UAE without a prescription. They'll generally be kept on the shelves alongside women's hygiene products. The price is comparable to Europe and Australasia.

## 10 Toilets

All shopping centres, five star hotels and good restaurants and bars have clean toilets – it's okay to walk off the street to use these. In shopping centres and cheaper street eateries you may come across "hole in the ground" Oriental toilets alongside Western toilets. You will also find bidets or a hose for ablutions.

*All restaurants charge municipality tax and service tax, which totals to 17.5 per cent.*

Left **Pedestrian crossing sign** Centre **A local bottled water brand** Right **A traffic policeman**

# Security & Health

### Precautions
The biggest danger to your health and wellbeing in the UAE is the heat. Take precautions to avoid dehydration, sunburn and sunstroke. From June to August in particular, avoid walking as much as possible and take advantage of the cheap air-conditioned taxis.

### Personal Safety
While petty crime is unheard of, be sensible – don't dress like a tourist and don't flash cash around. The most dangerous place is on the road. The UAE has one of the highest rates of road deaths on the planet. As a pedestrian be vigilant; drivers will not stop for you on a crossing, so cross only at lights where possible. If your taxi driver is driving too fast or recklessly, tell him to slow down.

### Drinking Water & Food Safety
The tap water is safe to drink. At most, you may experience an upset tummy for a couple of days as your body adjusts to new bacteria. When eating street food, only try eateries popular with locals.

### Consulates
Generally, embassies are in Abu Dhabi and consulates in Dubai, although there are a few exceptions. Check your consulate's UAE website for travel warnings and security information. Consulate phone numbers are listed in the Etisalat phone directory that is available in most hotel rooms.

### Emergency Info
In case of emergency, phone the following numbers: Police 999; Ambulance 998/999; Fire Department 997; Operator 181.

### If You Get Arrested
The UAE is an Islamic state and you can land in trouble for not respecting religious customs and decency laws. Under absolutely no condition drink alcohol and drive. In Sharjah, it's illegal for women to travel in a vehicle with men other than their husband. Women must dress modestly and not show their décolletage, upper arms or back. In Dubai and Abu Dhabi, arrests have resulted from foreigners being too affectionate in public, particularly during Ramadan. If you get arrested, do not sign anything in Arabic immediately. Your consulate should be your first call – they can help facilitate contact with a local bilingual lawyer.

### Road Traffic Accidents
If you're in an accident, first get out of harm's way, then call the police (999) for instructions. Do not move the car unless instructed to do so by the police. If another party is involved and you have your camera handy, take photos for insurance purposes.

### Hospitals
Hospital standards are outstanding in the UAE at both private and public hospitals. You will find that the service is faster at emergency departments at private hospitals. ✆ *Dubai: American Hospital 04 336 7777, Al Zahra Private Medical Centre 04 331 5000 • Abu Dhabi: Gulf Diagnostic Centre 02 665 8090, Centre Medical Franco-Emirien 02 626 5722*

### Dental
The UAE has excellent dentists and consultations are reasonably priced. ✆ *Dubai: British Dental Clinic 04 342 1318, American Dental Clinic 04 344 0668 • Abu Dhabi: British Dental Clinic 02 677 3308, Advanced Dental Clinic 02 681 2921*

### Pharmacies
There are many pharmacies in Dubai and Abu Dhabi that are open 24 hours. The daily newspapers list them. However, in Dubai, you can phone 04 223 2323 to find out the pharmacy nearest to you that's open, and in Abu Dhabi call 02 777 929.

*Global media surveys frequently place the UAE in the top 20 safest destinations.*

Left **Enjoy a walk through the Bastakiya** Right **An abra ride is a cheap way to cross the Creek**

# 🔟 Budget Tips

### When Not to Go
Avoid Dubai and Abu Dhabi during major events and conferences (unless it's something you actually want to go to!) when hotel room prices go through the roof. While December and January are the coolest months, winter is the peak season and hotels charge rack rates. Ramadan is another period to avoid.

### Summer Savings
While summer is best avoided due to the ferocious heat, this is the ideal time for budget travellers. Most hotels drop their rates by 50% and offer excellent holiday packages. The Summer Surprises shopping festival means there are great bargains to be found.

### Internet Deals
Travellers averse to package deals can find great deals on the Internet if they can be flexible. Accommodation websites such as Expedia offer great hotels at bargain prices, particularly in the quiet periods between big events and conferences. Hotel websites, such as the Accor site, are also a great source for discounted rooms.

### Transport
Budget travellers can save money by catching the abra across Dubai Creek. These open-sided wooden boats cost just AED 1 per trip and connect Dubai's main sights in Deira and Bur Dubai. The buses are a cheap alternative to taxis (see p103).

### Supermarkets
The supermarkets are excellent in the UAE. It's possible to find products from all over the world. Carrefour has a reputation for having the lowest prices. It also has the best bakery with delicious Middle Eastern pastries and an excellent deli counter where you buy olives, cheeses and cold meats for picnics and balcony snacks while you enjoy the sunset.

### Brunches & Buffets
The Friday Brunch is a ritual for many expats. Five star hotels offer great value all-you-can-eat-and-drink brunches, including alcohol, from AED 70–200 per person. Similar mid-week buffet lunches and dinners are also great value, starting from as low as AED 47. Check local magazines for the latest offers.

### Cheap Eats
A couple of shwarmas and a fresh mango juice make a great cheap eat. Shwarmas cost around AED 3 and juices from AED 6. If you're after something more filling, head to one of Dubai and Abu Dhabi's many cheap ethnic eateries (see p64) where you can spend as little as AED 30 per person for a curry or biryani or a few mezze dishes and a mixed Arabic grill.

### Happy Hours
While alcohol is expensive in the UAE (it's the only thing that is taxed), you can drink cheaply if you take advantage of happy hours (generally from 6pm–8pm) and drink promotions. Many bars and clubs offer half-price drinks, two-for-one deals, two free drinks or "free bubbly for the ladies", on particular nights.

### Free Stuff to Do
In Dubai, a walk through the Bastakiya or on Shindagha waterfront is free, while it costs nothing to stroll along Abu Dhabi's beautiful Corniche.

### Discounts & Bargaining
Bargaining is expected in the souqs and carpet shops. Make an offer at half the price and work up from there. In electronics and jewellery stores, it's acceptable to ask if that's the best price or for a discount if you pay cash or buy two. Let them know if you found something cheaper elsewhere and they'll probably drop their price.

 *Always keep small notes in your wallet when shopping.*

Left **A helpful concierge** Centre **Tipping etiquette** Right **Dress up well to eat out**

# Accommodation & Dining Tips

### 1 Hotel Taxes
The UAE is a tax-free country. However, visitors to the UAE can expect to pay a 10 per cent government tax and a 10 per cent service charge on hotel rooms.

### 2 Rooms
Hotel rooms in the UAE are spacious and also extremely secure. Most rooms are air-conditioned and come well equipped with television, telephones, minibar, tea and coffee facilities, toiletries and in-room safe. The best hotels also provide complimentary newspapers and bottled water.

### 3 Rack Rates & Discounts
While rack rates are quoted throughout this guide, they are rarely paid in the UAE. Travellers can book online through accommodation booking sites with considerably reduced discounts or book hotels as part of a package deal, while UAE residents can call hotels and request a residents discount.

### 4 Concierges
UAE concierges are generally excellent. They are a good source of local information and can recommend and book restaurants and organize transport and tours. They can also arrange to store your luggage if you have a late flight.

### 5 Extra costs
Extras that can add significantly to hotel room bills include phone calls and minibar costs. If you need to make lots of local phone calls, buy a local SIM card and phone card. While minibar prices are comparable to bar prices, you're better off buying duty free liquor.

### 6 Valet Parking
Almost all UAE hotels provide valet parking free-of-charge. Rarely will guests pay for valet parking if they're staying at a hotel, although there are exceptions. If you're staying in a mid-range or budget Deira hotel, you may have to park your car at a nearby parking station. The average cost is AED 20 per night. If you're hiring a car, contact your hotel ahead of time to enquire about parking facilities.

### 7 Tipping
In the UAE, it's customary to tip, although not obligatory. While most restaurants include a service charge, this doesn't always go to waiting staff. If the service was good, leave a tip, anything from 5–10 per cent. If it didn't meet your expectations, don't tip. Give porters a couple of dirhams per piece of luggage and if the taxi driver was friendly and helped with luggage, leave him a few coins.

### 8 Restaurant Reservations
Most hotels have "Restaurant Reservations" services. Take advantage of these to make your bookings, as there's nothing as tedious as having to visit half a dozen eateries before you find a table. Restaurants fill quickly in Dubai and Abu Dhabi and it can be hard to get a table on weekends. Make bookings as far in advance as possible.

### 9 Meal Times
UAE residents and locals eat late compared to North American, British and Australasian diners. Arab expats and Emiratis tend to book restaurant tables from 10pm onwards, while European expats eat around 8:30pm–9pm. Eat any earlier and you'll miss out on the fun – you'll only be dining with other tourists.

### 10 Dress Codes
Good restaurants require smart-casual to formal dress in the UAE. Emiratis wear their best *dishdashas* and *abayas*, while expats dress up too – even in casual restaurants, women will look glam while men will wear trousers (never jeans) and a long sleeved shirt. In fine dining restaurants, a smart suit jacket is expected (although a tie is sometimes optional).

**Price Categories**

| | | |
|---|---|---|
| For a standard, double room per night (with breakfast if included), taxes and extra charges. | **D** | Under AED 365 |
| | **DD** | AED 365–550 |
| | **DDD** | AED 550–730 |
| | **DDDD** | AED 730–1100 |
| | **DDDDD** | Over AED 1100 |

Ibis World Trade Centre lobby

# 🔟 Cheap Accommodation: Dubai

### 1 Ibis World Trade Centre Hotel

One of Dubai's best bargains, the Ibis offers small, clean and stylish rooms. The catch, however, is that there's no service or extras for this price – don't expect someone to help with your bags. But there's internet access, wireless in the public spaces, and the hotel restaurant, Cubo, offers decent Italian fare. ⦸ *Map E6 • Next to Dubai Convention and Exhibition Centre, Sheikh Zayed Rd • 04 332 4444 • www. accor.com • DD*

### 2 Holiday Inn Express

This new budget hotel is right in the middle of Dubai's media hub (Internet City, Media City and Knowledge Village) and makes a great base for exploring New Dubai. Rooms and facilities are generous for the price. ⦸ *Map B2 • Knowledge Village, New Dubai • 04 427 5555 • www.hiexpress.com • DD*

### 3 Al Hijaz Motel

Book here for a real taste of heritage flavour. Located on the Deira side of the Creek, Al Hijaz has spacious, traditionally styled rooms in a renovated courtyard building. ⦸ *Map K1 • Near Al Ahmadia School, Deira souq • 04 225 0085 • www. alhijazmotel.com • DD*

### 4 Residence Deira by Le Meridien

Dubai's best value and most central budget accommodation is a hidden gem. It offers the most professional service of any budget accommodation in Dubai. The spacious studio apartments include satellite TV and small kitchenettes. ⦸ *Map L2 • Riggat Al Buteen, Deira • 04 224 1777 • www. lemeridien.com • DD*

### 5 Capitol Hotel

Well-located on Mina Rd, this decent mid-range is ideal for those who want to experience it all – the old and new Dubai – and don't plan on spending much time at the hotel. If you do, you're in for nightclub noise and smoke even in the non-smoking rooms. ⦸ *Map F4 • Al Mina Rd, Satwa • 04 346 0111 • www.capitol-hotel.com • DD*

### 6 Pacific Hotel

Close to the shopping action of Deira's souqs and Baniyas Square, this budget hotel's simple rooms have satellite TV and balconies, but the main draw is the location. ⦸ *Map L2 • Al Sabkha Rd, Deira • 04 227 6700 • www.pacifichotel-dubai.com • DD*

### 7 Hotel Florida International

Situated in one of the most modern buildings in this area, this is also one of the cleanest of Deira's budget hotels. While the rooms are basic, they come with satellite TV. It's a short stroll away from Baniyas Square. ⦸ *Map L1 • Al Sabkha Rd, Deira • 04 224 7777 • www.florahotels.ae • D*

### 8 Ramee Hotel Apartments

In a bustling street of Bur Dubai, these spacious, clean hotel apartments are great value. They are equipped with satellite television and include kitchenettes with fridge, stovetop, microwave and washing machine. The undercover parking is an advantage in this area. ⦸ *Map J2 • Al Rolla Rd, Bur Dubai • 04 642 2696 • www.ramee-group.com • D*

### 9 Sun and Sand Hotel

This central Deira hotel offers daily shuttle buses to Jumeirah's beaches. There's also a rooftop pool. ⦸ *Map L4 • Off Maktoum Rd, Deira • 04 223 9000 • www. sunsandhotel.com • D*

### 10 Dubai Youth Hostel

Dubai's only youth hostel may not be central but it offers cheap and clean hotel-style accommodation in its new building, and basic dorm-like accommodation in the old building. ⦸ *Map F2 • Al Nahda Rd, near Al Qusais • 04 298 8151 • uaeyha@ emirates.net.ae • D*

*The budget hotels are mostly occupied with male traders. Women travelling unaccompanied may feel uncomfortable.*

Left **Novotel Centre Hotel** Centre **HJ Diplomat Hotel signboard** Right **Al Maha Rotana Suites**

# Inexpensive Hotels: Abu Dhabi

### 1 Al Maha Rotana Suites

Abu Dhabi's best value accommodation is on the bustling Hamdan St, with access to shops, cinemas and interesting views of the city. ❧ *Map P2 • Hamdan St • 02 610 6666 • www.rotana.com • DD*

### 2 Hilton Corniche Residence

This rather conservative Hilton is a favourite with business travellers who love its personal service, high-speed internet access, wi-fi and the stunning sea views. ❧ *Map P6 • Corniche Rd, Central • 02 627 6000 • www.hilton.com • DD*

### 3 Hilton Baynunah Hotel

The spacious, well-equipped suites and executive apartments in this 42-storey blue glass tower have fabulous views over the city. ❧ *Map N3 • Corniche West • 02 632 7777 • www. hilton.com • DD*

### 4 Novotel Centre Hotel

Centrally located, this hotel looks worn around the edges and smells of smoke, but is popular with package tourists and airline crew. The low-ceilinged rooms can feel claustrophobic and the tiny windows don't take advantage of the city views. ❧ *Map P2 • Hamdan St • 02 633 3555 • www.novotel.com • DD*

### 5 Howard Johnson Diplomat Hotel

With several bars and clubs on site, this hotel sees a lot of action in the evenings, but isn't really suitable for families. The spacious rooms are not particularly clean, but have good coffee-making facilities. It's also one of the few hotels in the city to allow pets. ❧ *Map P4 • Khalifa St • 02 671 0000 • www.hojo.com • DD*

### 6 Grand Continental Flamingo Hotel

This shiny glass tower has shops and cinemas at its doorstep and the Corniche a couple of blocks away. The rooms are spacious and executive suites have kitchenettes. Rooms on high floors have fantastic views. Service, while efficient, can be impersonal. ❧ *Map P2 • Hamdan St • 02 626 2200 • www.grand-continental-flamingo.com • D*

### 7 Al Ain Palace Hotel

With the elegant Royal Meridien towering above it, you'd expect the Al Ain Palace to have an inferiority complex. Yet, this friendly hotel is home to some of the best restaurants, making it an attractive option for those who don't feel like heading out after a hot day's sightseeing. ❧ *Map N2 • Corniche Road East • 02 679 4777 • www.alain-palacehotel.com • DD*

### 8 Al Diar Capital Hotel

Slightly more upmarket than its nearby sister hotels, the Capital is nowhere near the quality you'd expect from the five star classification it has. More of a mid-range business hotel, it represents a good deal only if you can get it for mid-range prices off the web or as part of a package. ❧ *Map N1 • Meena Rd • 02 678 7700 • www. aldiarhotels.com • DDD*

### 9 Al Diar Regency Hotel

Located close to Hamdan Street, this hotel has tinted-mirror and marble-tiled lobbies that seek to impress. Unfortunately, the decor in the rooms is tacky. However, the rooms are clean and have cooking facilities. Women should avoid the hotel's bars if unaccompanied. ❧ *Map N1 • Meena Rd • 02 676 5000 • www. aldiarhotels.com • DD*

### 10 Al Diar Mina

While Al Diar's Mina property is very similar in quality to the chain's Regency hotel, Al Mina's rooms are more expensive. It is centrally situated and guests can use the facilities at the Regency. The one advantage Al Mina has over the Regency is its splendid sea views. ❧ *Map N1 • Meena Rd • 02 678 1000 • www. aldiarhotels.com • DDD*

**Price Categories**

For a standard, double room per night (with breakfast if included), taxes and extra charges.

| | |
|---|---|
| **D** | Under AED 365 |
| **DD** | AED 365–550 |
| **DDD** | AED 550–730 |
| **DDDD** | AED 730–1100 |
| **DDDDD** | Over AED 1100 |

Left **Traditional decor at the Orient Guest House** Right **The Rihab Rotana Suites emblem**

# 🔟 Mid-Priced Hotels: Dubai

### 1 XVA
This elegant hotel in a restored courtyard house is full of atmosphere. The stylish hotel rooms are minimalist in design. Don't expect any extras here; but who needs them when you can hear the call-to-prayer echoing through the streets. ✆ Map K2 • Bastakiya • 04 353 5383 • www.xvagallery.com • DDDD

### 2 Al Bustan Rotana
The airport location seems to keep this outstanding five star hotel's pricing well below other hotels of similar quality. Rooms are spacious and well-equipped. The hotel is also home to some of the city's best eateries. ✆ Map L6 • Garhoud, near Dubai International Airport • 04 282 0000 • www.rotana.com • DDDD

### 3 Rihab Rotana Suites
Five minutes from Dubai International Airport and a few minutes walk from Deira City Centre mall, these sleek contemporary suites on a busy road are ideal for business travellers and couples. The spacious rooms with well-equipped kitchenettes and all mod cons, are excellent value. If you can't face another meal out, there's a café downstairs. ✆ Map L5 • Garhoud, next to City Centre • 04 294 0300 • www.rotana.com • DDDD

### 4 Orient Guest House
This delightful boutique hotel is situated in a renovated courtyard building in the historic Bastakiya area. The traditional rooms with high ceilings are decorated in Arabian and Indian decor. The quiet courtyards are wonderful for relaxing in after a hot day's sightseeing. ✆ Map K2 • Al Fahidi Roundabout, Bur Dubai • 04 351 9111 • www.arabian-courtyard.com • DDD

### 5 Rydges Plaza
Not exactly central, this old hotel is still popular with Australian and British travellers. The clean rooms are somewhat cramped, but come well equipped. ✆ Map E4 • Satwa Roundabout, Satwa • 04 398 2222 • www.rydges.com • DDDD

### 6 Four Points Sheraton
Conveniently located for Bur Dubai souqs, Dubai Museum, the Bastakiya and Bur Juman shopping, this standard hotel is popular with business travellers and tourists on stopovers. ✆ Map J2 • Khalid Bin Al-Waleed Rd • 04 397 7444 • www.starwood.com • DDD

### 7 Marco Polo Hotel
This excellent 4-star may seem like it's off the beaten track, but it's only a 10-minute taxi ride from the airport and a 15-minute stroll to the fascinating *dhow* wharves or Deira souqs. The hotel has a couple of excellent restaurants. ✆ Map M2 • Al-Mateena St, Deira • 04 272 0000 • www.marcopolohotel.net • DDDD

### 8 Moscow Hotel
In an excellent Deira location, this Russian-themed hotel is (obviously) popular with Russian package tourists. The boldly painted rooms are spacious and comfortable. ✆ Map L3 • Al Maktoum Rd, Deira • 04 228 8222 • www.moscow-hoteldubai.com • DDD

### 9 Regent Palace Hotel
Opposite the swish Bur Juman shopping centre, this hotel has a great location. While the rooms are comfortable, they're in need of renovation. ✆ Map J3 • Sheikh Khalifa Bin Zayed Rd, Bur Dubai • 04 396 3888 • www.ramee-group.com • DDDD

### 10 Regal Plaza Hotel
A short stroll from Bur Dubai souqs, Dubai Museum and the wonderful Bastakiya, and next door to electronics mall Al Ain Shopping Centre, this decent hotel is fine if you're only after a bed for the night. Don't head here for rest or recreation, as it tends to get noisy. ✆ Map J2 • Al Mankhool Rd, Bur Dubai • 04 355 6633 • www.ramee-group.com • DDDD

*Look online for the best deals on hotel rates.*

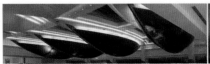 

Left **Dhow** bottoms in the Grand Hyatt Dubai ceiling Right **The elegant Sheraton Dubai Creek**

# Creek View Hotels: Dubai

**1 Park Hyatt Dubai**
This white Moroccan-inspired low-rise hotel is situated on one of the most sublime spots on Dubai Creek, overlooking the attractive marina and yacht club. ⊛ Map K5 • Dubai Creek Golf & Yacht Club, Deira • 04 602 1234 • www.dubai.park.hyatt. com • DDDDD

**2 InterContinental Dubai Festival City**
One of the latest of a string of high-profile hotel openings, the new InterContinental at Dubai Festival City is a chic property, with superb attention to detail and well-drilled staff on hand throughout the hotel's vast amenities. Creek-view rooms have breath-taking vistas. ⊛ Map E3 • Dubai Festival City, Deira • 04 701 1111 • www. intercontinental.com • DDDDD

**3 Sheraton Dubai Creek**
About as close to the Creek as you can get, it's as if you're right on top of the shimmering water when you're in the elegant rooms at this striking hotel. ⊛ Map K3 • Baniyas Rd, Deira • 04 228 1111 • www.starwood.com • DDDD

**4 Hilton Dubai Creek**
Make sure to book a Creek view room for the best birds-eye-view of Dubai's bustling waterway. This Carlos Ott-designed hotel is one of Dubai's most stylish, with a striking exterior and a sleek black marble interior. ⊛ Map L3 • Baniyas Rd, Deira • 04 227 1111 • www.hilton.com • DDDDD

**5 Grand Hyatt Dubai**
This massive property may have marvellous views over Creekside Park across to the Dubai Creek Golf & Yacht Club, but it's easy to let the myriad attractions within the hotel distract you. There's a wonderful interior rainforest garden with dhow bottoms embedded in the ceiling and myriad bars and restaurants. ⊛ Map J6 • Al Qataiyat Rd, Bur Dubai • 04 317 1234 • www.dubai. grand.hyatt.com • DDDDD

**6 Radisson SAS Dubai Creek Hotel**
While the rooms here are comfortable and there are Creek views from the small balconies, the design doesn't take advantage enough of its wonderful waterside location. ⊛ Map K2 • Baniyas Rd, Deira • 04 222 7171 • www. radissonsas.com • DDDDD

**7 Carlton Tower Hotel**
With views of the Creek that are just as stunning as those from the Riviera next door, you'll pay more for a room at the Carlton because of its big swimming pool. And you probably won't regret it after a sweaty day in Dubai's heat. ⊛ Map L2 • Baniyas Rd, Deira • 04 222 7111 • www. carltontower.net • DDDD

**8 Riviera Hotel**
This is one of Dubai's best-located hotels for sightseeing. It's a short stroll to Deira's many souqs, while the fascinating dhow docks are just across the road. ⊛ Map K2 • Baniyas Rd, Deira • 04 222 2131 • riviera@emirates.net.ae • DDD

**9 Arabian Courtyard Hotel & Spa**
The fine views from the Arabian Courtyard are some of Dubai's most fascinating. The Arabian-inspired rooms are spacious and the staff is friendly. ⊛ Map J2 • Al Fahidi St, opposite Dubai Museum, Bur Dubai • 04 351 9111 • www.arabian-courtyard.com • DDD

**10 Hyatt Regency**
Stunningly situated and recently renovated, the Grand Hyatt has spectacular views over the Arabian Sea. It has one of the most atmospheric lobbies, with palm trees, mashrabiya screened balconies and glass feature floors with sand beneath them. ⊛ Map L1 • Al Khaleej Rd, Deira • 04 676 5000 • www.dubai.regency.hyatt. com • DD

**Price Categories**

| | | |
|---|---|---|
| For a standard, | **D** | Under AED 365 |
| double room per | **DD** | AED 365–550 |
| night (with breakfast | **DDD** | AED 550–730 |
| if included), taxes | **DDDD** | AED 730–1100 |
| and extra charges. | **DDDDD** | Over AED 1100 |

Left **The beach at the Meridien Mina Seyahi**

# 🔟 Luxury Beach Resorts: Dubai

**1 Burj Al Arab**
Dramatically jutting into the sea, Dubai's iconic "seven-star" property provides the ultimate in personal attention – from your arrival in a Rolls Royce, to the staff greeting you in the flamboyant foyer with welcome refreshments, cold towels, incense and dates, to the personal butler in your duplex suite. The interior is gaudy but the spectacular coastal views, especially from the Skyview Bar, make up for it *(see pp16–17).*

**2 One&Only Royal Mirage**
One of the world's most romantic resorts, this is an exotic Moroccan-inspired resort set in lush palm-filled gardens with serene ponds. The white sand beach is lined with elegant white umbrellas and regal private VIP canopies overlooking the Palm Island development *(see p44).*

**3 Al Qasr**
The opulent Al Qasr ("the palace" in Arabic) is graced with enormous wooden doors, graceful arches and Moroccan stonework. You'll find mashrabiya screens, Moroccan lamps and terracotta urns all over the place. There's a gorgeous white sand beach and great views of Mina A'Salam and Burj Al Arab *(see pp18–19).*

**4 Mina A'Salam**
The old-Arabian architecture of Mina A'Salam is inspired by the ancient towers of Yemen and Saudi Arabia as well as by the local wind-tower architecture of Dubai's Bastakiya area. The rooms feature rich upholsteries, inlaid furniture, Oriental lamps and Arabesque patterned prints and tiles. The lattice balconies overlook the manmade waterways and splendid palm-lined beach *(see pp18–19).*

**5 Grosvenor House**
The well-appointed rooms at this swanky hotel are spacious with stunning marina or sea views. Guests can use the white sand beach and access water activities at its sister hotel across the road, the Royal Meridien. ⊗ *Map B2 • Dubai Marina • 04 399 8888 • www.grosvenor-house-dubai.com • DDDDD*

**6 Ritz Carlton**
This sumptuous hotel lives up to the reputation of this renowned chain, with lots of marble, chandeliers, Persian carpets and fresh flowers everywhere. Its palm-filled gardens and white sand beach are outstanding *(see p44).*

**7 Le Meridien Mina Seyahi Resort**
Indulge in a wide range of beach activities and water sports from windsurfing and wake-boarding to sailing and deep-sea fishing. There are several swimming pools and also a complimentary kid's "Penguin Club" *(see p44).*

**8 Jumeirah Beach Hotel**
While the interiors of this wave-shaped hotel are rather gaudy when compared with Dubai's chic new hotels, families love the bright, bold colours, excellent beach facilities and myriad kids activities *(see p44).*

**9 Le Royal Meridien Beach Resort**
Dubai's most elegant Jumeirah Beach accommodation also has the most sunbathing space. You won't miss out on a sun bed, as the resort has several swimming pools *(see p44).*

**10 Dubai Marine Beach Resort & Spa**
Holidaymakers who like to sunbathe by day and party by night will love this resort. There are lush landscaped gardens, several swimming pools and a lovely, albeit small, white sand beach, while close by is Dubai's most stylish bar, Sho Cho's, one of its hippest clubs, Boudoir, and several good restaurants. ⊗ *Map E4 • Jumeirah Beach Rd, adjoining Palm Strip • 04 346 1111 • www.dxmarine. com • DDDD*

Left **Emirates Palace** Centre **Millennium Hotel lobby** Right **The Beach Rotana swimming pool**

# Luxury Resorts: Abu Dhabi

### Emirates Palace
Choose from amongst the Coral, Pearl and Diamond Rooms, Khaleej Suites or Palace Suites. All the rooms feature wide plasma screen TVs and extras such as welcome cocktails, flowers and fruit in the room, butler service, complimentary minibar and internet access *(see pp22–3)*.

### Le Royal Meridien
While all the rooms are beautifully appointed and have sublime views of the Corniche and Arabian Sea, the Royal Club rooms are worth the extra dirhams for the Hermes products alone. *Map N2 • Khalifa St • 02 695 0415 • www.lemeridien.com • DDDDD*

### Shangri-La Qaryat Al Beri
This new Shangri-La is a superb hotel with rooms overlooking water, a long private beach and several swimming pools. It also has a spa, restaurants and a shopping centre. *Qaryat Al Beri • 02 509 8888 • www.shangri-la.com • DDDDD*

### Beach Rotana Hotel
While the well-appointed rooms are comfortable and come with good facilities, the attraction at this splendid hotel is the white sand beach and the popular PADI dive school. Dine at one of the many excellent restaurants, then join the locals for coffee late in the evening at the lobby. *Map Q1 • Tourist Club area • 02 644 3000 • www.rotana.com • DDDDD*

### Millennium Hotel
This swanky hotel has elegant expansive rooms with splendid views over the Corniche and Lulu Island and out to sea. Ideally positioned for sightseeing, the small swimming pool is a disappointment. *Map N2 • Khalifa St • 02 626 2700 • www.millenniumhotels.com • DDDDD*

### Le Meridien
The rooms here are very plush, with velvet upholstery and dark wood. The interactive TVs and high speed internet make this hotel ideal for business travellers. The highlight, however, is the Meridien Village, with 15 restau-rants and bars set in lush tropical gardens. *Map P1 • Tourist Club area • 02 644 6666 • www.lemeridien.com • DDDD*

### Sheraton Abu Dhabi Resort & Towers
There are good water and leisure activities here and the beachside sheesha spot is lovely. Eat at the excellent restaurants on site. *Map N1 • Corniche Rd East, Tourist Club area • 02 677 3333 • www.sheraton.com/abudhabi • DDDDD*

### InterContinental Abu Dhabi
The hotel overlooks the beautiful marina and has a fine white sand beach. A long refurbishment programme is currently underway to ensure that their restaurants and bars are about to get even better! *Map P6 • Al Bateen area • 02 681 1900 • DDDD*

### Hilton International Abu Dhabi
Long a favourite of Abu Dhabi's expats for its excellent restaurants and bars, holidaymakers love the hotel's beautiful swimming pools and Breakwater beach, lined with shady palm trees, and myriad water sports. Rooms are spacious and comfortable and come with many little extras. *Map P6 • Corniche Rd West • 02 681 1900 • www.hilton.com • DDDD*

### Sheraton Khalidiya Hotel
After a recent and long overdue refurbishment, the Sheraton Khalidiya now has plush, comfortable rooms to rival the city's very best hotels. The spacious suites have separate living and dining areas, all rooms have wireless internet access, and most have wonderful views over the city and out to sea. *Map P4 • Corniche Rd West Khalidiya • 02 644 4739 • www.sheraton.com/khalidiya • DDDD*

*Business travellers should ask hotels for corporate rates, which are considerably less than rack rates.*

**Price Categories**

For a standard, | **D** Under AED 365
double room per | **DD** AED 365–550
night (with breakfast | **DDD** AED 550–730
if included), taxes | **DDDD** AED 730–1100
and extra charges. | **DDDDD** Over AED 1100

Left **Kempinski Hotel reception** Right **The Thai experience at Dusit Dubai**

# TOP10 Business & City Hotels: Dubai

### Raffles Dubai
The Middle East's first Raffles combines warmth and luxury with impeccable service. Its enormous rooms have great views from the distinctive Egyptian-style pyramid building, which gels with the Wafi shopping complex. The hotel's restaurant, Fire & Ice *(see p71)*, has become one of the city's best. ✎ *Map H6 • Sheikh Rashis Rd • 04 324 8888 • www.raffles.com • DDDD*

### Jumeirah Emirates Towers
This elegant hotel's lobby is one of the city's most vibrant, especially in the evenings. Adjoining the hotel is the chic Boulevard shopping centre with excellent eateries and bars *(see p36)*.

### Kempinski Hotel
A contemporary city style hotel, it offers a swish alternative to the beach resorts. The hotel is attached to Mall of the Emirates' indoor snow park, Ski Dubai *(see p32)*. The well-equipped rooms are spacious and very swanky. ✎ *Map C2 • Sheikh Zayed Rd, Interchange 4, Al Barsha • 04 340 3392 • www.kempinski.com • DDDDD*

### Radisson SAS Dubai Media City
This smart new hotel in the centre of Dubai Media City is ideal for those doing business

here or for tourists looking for an alternative to the beach experience – Dubai Marina, Mall of the Emirates and Ibn Battuta Mall are nearby. ✎ *Map B2 • Dubai Media City • 04 390 0070 • www.media-city.dubai.radissonsas.com • DDDDD*

### Dusit Dubai
What sets the Dusit apart is its gentle welcoming Thai hospitality, from the "Sawadee-ka" greeting to the Thai canapés. The spacious rooms cater well to the business traveller, but it's worth paying extra for Club Rooms, that come with enticing perks. ✎ *Map C6 • Sheikh Zayed Rd • 04 343 3333 • www.dusit.com • DDDDD*

### Fairmont
Conveniently located for business, shopping and sightseeing, the hotel's architecture and plush rooms ooze style. ✎ *Map E5 • Sheikh Zayed Rd • 04 332 5555 • www.fairmont.com • DDDD*

### Shangri-La
Known as the hotel where Hollywood's stars choose to stay – George Clooney and Matt Damon did so when making the movie *Syriana* – this is one of Dubai's swankiest, with a dramatic lobby, posh rooms and splendid restaurants. ✎ *Map C5 • Sheikh Zayed Rd • 04 343 8888 • www.shangri-la.com • DDDDD*

### Novotel World Trade Centre
The rooms, though comfortable, are cramped (by Dubai standards) and not very well equipped. The public spaces are stylish, however, and the lobby café is great for business meetings. The convenient location is the biggest plus here. ✎ *Map E6 • Adjoining Dubai Convention and Exhibition Centre, off Sheikh Zayed Rd • 04 332 0000 • www.accor.com • DDDD*

### Towers Rotana Hotel
Predominantly aimed at the business traveller, this is a comfortable hotel in the heart of Sheikh Zayed Rd, and just 5 minutes from the Convention and Exhibition Centre and the World Trade Centre. There's a good gym on the premises, as well as a large swimming pool. ✎ *Map D5 • Sheikh Zayed Rd • 04 343 8000 • www.rotana.com • DDDD*

### Al Murooj Rotana Hotel & Suites
This is a popular Mediterranean-style hotel. Regular guests like the comfortable rooms and personable but professional service, while expats have taken a liking to the many relaxed restaurants and cafés on site. ✎ *Map D6 • Just off Sheikh Zayed Rd near Defence Roundabout • 04 321 1111 • www.rotana.com • DDDDD*

*"Club" rooms come with extras such as use of the "Club Lounge", meeting rooms, afternoon tea, pre-dinner drinks and canapés.*

# General Index

# Acknowledgements

## The Authors

LARA DUNSTON was an Abu Dhabi resident of five years and Dubai resident of three. Lara has authored several guides to Dubai and the UAE, and scores of travel features for magazines and newspapers around the world.

SARAH MONAGHAN lived in Dubai for five years where she edited its leading glossy women's magazine, *Emirates Woman*. The former editor of *Everything Spain Magazine* and currently of *Gabon Magazine*, she now contributes travel features to national and international publications.

TERRY CARTER specializes in travel photography and his work has featured in guidebooks and magazines across the globe. A former Dubai and Abu Dhabi resident, he's often back shooting in these cities and loves the clear light and friendliness of the multicultural population.

AT DORLING KINDERSLEY

**Publisher**
Douglas Amrine

**Publishing Manager**
Sadie Smith

**Design Manager**
Jane Ewart

**Project Art Editor**
Sonal Bhatt

**Senior Cartographic Designers**
Casper Morris, Suresh Kumar

**Cartographer**
Jasneet Kaur

**DTP Designer**
Natasha Lu

**Production**
Rita Sinha

**Photographer**
Terry Carter

**Fact checking**
Debbie Rooke

**Additional Photography**
Sonal Bhatt, Peter Cornelissen

**Maps**
Base mapping for Dubai City, Greater Dubai and Abu Dhabi derived from Netmaps.

**Picture Credits**
t=top; tc=top centre; tr=top right; cla=centre left above; ca=centre above; cra=centre right above; cl=centre left; c=centre; cr=centre right; clb=centre left below; cb=centre below; crb=centre right below; bl=bottom left; bc=bottom centre; br=bottom right.

The photographer, writers and publisher would like to thank the media staff at the following sights and organizations for their helpful cooperation:

One&Only Royal Mirage; Jumeirah International; Emirates Palace and Kempinski Mall of the Emirates; Grosvenor House, Le Royal Meridien, Meridien, Sheraton Hotels and Starwood Group; Radisson SAS Dubai Media City and Deira Hotels; Park Hyatt Dubai, Grand Hyatt Dubai and Hyatt International;

Fairmont Hotel; Dusit Dubai; Arabian Courtyard Hotel and Spa; Marco Polo Hotel; Al Tayer Group; The Rotana Group, Abu Dhabi Beach Rotana, Al Maha Rotana and Dubai Towers Rotana Hotel; Abu Dhabi Millennium Hotel; Sho Cho and Dubai Marine Beach Resort and Spa; Zinc at the Crowne Plaza Hotel; Wafi City & Cleopatra's Spa; Sheikh Mohammed Centre for Cultural Understanding; Dubai Museum; Dubai Cultural Foundation; Arabian Adventures; Ski Dubai; Time Machine Group; Luca Gagliardi and Gordon Ramsey's Verre; Sheikh Maisa Al Qassimi and the Amzaan staff; The Third Line; 9714; B21 Gallery; Basta Art Cafe; XVA; Art Space; Lata's; Mumbai Se; Ginger and Lace; Villa Moda; National Iranian Carpets; Pride of Kashmir; Al Jaber Gallery; Anita Daga and InterContinental Hotel Group; Mark Fuller and Embassy; and Stephanie Khouy and Raffles Dubai.

Every effort has been made to trace the copyright holders, and we apologize in advance for any unintentional omissions. We would be pleased to insert the appropriate acknowledgements in any subsequent edition of this publication.

4CORNERSIMAGES: SIME/ Schmid Reinhard 56-7.

ALAMY: G P Bowater 54b; JON ARNOLD IMAGES: Gavin Hellier 1c; Eric Nathan 7cra.

BALLOON ADVENTURES DUBAI: 50br.

NAKHEEL BRANDHUB: 32b.

CORBIS: Georgina Bowater 28-9; Jose Fuste Raga 6bc; 4-5; 86-7.

DEPARTMENT OF TOURISM AND COMMERCE MARKETING: Photographs provided courtesy of the Government of Dubai, 32tr; 33tr.

DUBAI AUTODROME LLC: 50tr.

GETTY IMAGES: Hugh Sitton 3br.

SIR BANIYAS & SAADIYAT ISLAND: © TDIC 32tl, 32tc.

JOHN WEISS: © www.tsca.net, 2003 10cla.

All other images © Dorling Kindersley.

For further information see: www.dkimages.com.

## Special Editions of DK Travel Guides

DK Travel Guides can be purchased in bulk quantities at discounted prices for use in promotions or as premiums. We are also able to offer special editions and personalized jackets, corporate imprints and excerpts from all of our books, tailored specifically to meet your own needs.

To find out more, please contact:

(in the United States) **SpecialSales@ dk.com**

(in the UK) **Sarah.Burgess@dk.com**

(in Canada) DK Special Sales at **general@tourmaline.ca**

(in Australia) **business.development@ pearson.com.au**

# Phrase Book

## In an Emergency

| | |
|---|---|
| Help! | Enje**doo**ni |
| Stop | **Wak**-kaf |
| Can you call a doctor? | **Mom**kin **tat**lob ta**beeb**? |
| Can you call an ambulance? | **Mom**kin **tat**lob el es'**aaf**? |
| Can you call the police? | **Mom**kin **tat**lob el **shor**ta? |
| Can you call the fire brigade? | **Mom**kin **tat**lob el et**faa**? |
| Where is the nearest hospital? | Wayn **ag**rab mos**tash**fa? |
| Is there a telephone here? | Ako tele**foon** **hu**na? |

## Useful Words and Phrases

| | |
|---|---|
| Yes | **Na**-am |
| No | Laa |
| Hello | Sa**laam** a**lai**kum |
| Goodbye | **Ma**'aa al sa**laa**ma |
| See you later | **E**la al le**kaa** |
| Excuse me | **'Af**wan |
| Sorry (said by man) | **Aa**sif |
| Sorry (said by woman) | **Aa**sifa |
| Thank you | Shake**reen** |
| Please | Luw **tas**ma'h |
| | |
| Peace be upon you | Al sa**laam** 'a**lai**kum |
| Peace be upon you (as response) | A**lai**kum al sa**laam** |
| Good morning | Sa**baa**'h al khayr |
| Good evening | Ma**saa**-o al khayr |
| Good night | Tosbi**hoo**na **a**la khayr |
| Pleased to meet you | Ya ah**leen** |
| How are you? | Keef al 'haal? |
| I'm fine | Zeen |
| | |
| I don't understand | Ma **af**ham |
| What did he say? | **She**nu kaal? |
| Do you speak English? | **Ta**'hki enk**lee**zi? |
| Does anyone speak English? | Aku '**ha**da ye'**h**kee enk**lee**zi? |
| | |
| Have you got a table for...? | Aku **taa**wila hug ...? |
| I would like to reserve a table | A**reed** a'**h**jiz **taa**wila |
| Can I have the bill please? | Al 'he**saab** luw **tas**ma'h |
| I am vegetarian | **Ana** na**baa**ti |
| | |
| God willing | In**shaa**l-la |
| No problem | **Maa**fi **mosh**kila |
| | |
| big | ka**beer** |
| small | sa**gee**r |
| hot | '**haar** |
| cold | **baa**rid |
| bad | say-**ye**'e |
| good | tay-**yeb** |
| open | maf**too**'h |
| closed | me**sak**-kar |
| on the right | '**a**la al ya**meen** |
| on the left | '**a**la al ya**saar** |
| near | ka**reeb** |
| far | ba'**eed** |
| men's toilet | twa**let** hug al re**jaal** |
| ladies' toilet | twa**let** hug al '**ha**reem |
| a little | ka**leel** |
| a lot | **waaj**ed |

## Making a Telephone Call

| | |
|---|---|
| Hello | A**loo** |
| I'd like to speak to... | A**reed** akal-**lim** ... |
| This is... | **A**na ... |
| I'll call back later | **Raa**'h at-**ta**sal ba'a**deen** |
| Please say ... called | Khab-**bir**ho **an**-na ... et-**ta**sal |

## In a Hotel

| | |
|---|---|
| hotel | **fon**dok |
| Do you have a room? | La**day**kom '**hoj**ra? |
| I have a reservation | **En**di 'hajz |
| With bathroom | Bee 'ham-**maam** |
| single room | '**hoj**ra far**diy**-ya |
| double room | '**hoj**ra le et**neen** |
| porter | na**toor** |
| shower | dosh |
| key | mef**taa**'h |

## Sightseeing

| | |
|---|---|
| art gallery | **ma**'arad luw'**haat** fan**ey**-ya |
| beach | **shaa**te'e |
| bus station | **muw**gaf el **baah**s |
| district | **men**takaa |
| entrance | **mad**khal |
| exit | **makh**raj |
| garden | '**ha**deeka |
| guide | **mor**shid |
| guided tour | **mor**shid al **juw**la |
| map | **khaar**ta |
| mosque | **jaa**me'a |
| museum | **mut**'haf |
| park | mota**naz**-zah |
| river | **na**her |
| taxi | **tak**si |
| ticket | **tath**kara |
| tourist office | **mak**tab se**yaa**'hi |
| Please put the (taxi) meter on | Luw **tas**ma'h, **daw**-war al '**ad**-daad |
| How much is it to...? | Kam raa'h te**kal**-lafni **e**la ...? |
| Please take me to (this address) | **Khoth**ni **e**la (**haa**za al 'on**waan**) |

## Shopping

| | |
|---|---|
| How much is it? | Kam floos? |
| I'd like... | A**reed** |
| This one | **Haa**za |
| Do you accept credit cards? | Hal takba**loon** **kre**dit kaard? |
| That's too much | **Haa**za **waay**ed |
| I'll give you... | **A**na raa'h a'a**teek** ... |
| I'll take it | Raa'h **aakh**doh |
| market | sook |
| expensive | **ghaa**li |
| cheap | ra**khee**s |
| chemist's | sayda**laa**ni |

## Menu Decoder

| | |
|---|---|
| 'aish | rice |
| 'a**seer** | fruit juice |
| be**doon** | without |
| bee | with |
| **bee**ra | beer |
| beez | egg |
| beez mas**look** | hard-boiled egg |
| be**riaa**ni al da**jaa**j | chicken biryani |
| be**riaa**ni al **la**hem | meat biryani |
| be**riaa**ni al ro**biaa**n | shrimp biryani |

*When you see an ' in the Arabic, this means that you pronounce the letter after it with a little puff of air.*